ENLIGHTENMENT
without
GOD

Mandukya Upanishad

ENLIGHTENMENT
without
GOD

Mandukya Upanishad

SWAMI RAMA

HONESDALE, PENNSYLVANIA USA

Himalayan Institute
952 Bethany Turnpike
Honesdale, PA 18431

HimalayanInstitute.org

©1982 by Himalayan International Institute of Yoga Science and
Philosophy of the U.S.A.®

All rights reserved.

No part of this book in any manner, in whole or in part,
in English or in any other language, may be reproduced
or transmitted in any form or by any means, electronic or
mechanical, including photocopying and recording, or by any
information storage or retrieval system without prior written
permission of the copyright owner.

Printed in the United States of America

27 26 25 24 23   8 9 10 11 12

ISBN-13: 978-0-89389-084-1 (paper)

Library of Congress Catalog Card Number 82083391

This paper meets the requirements of ANSI/NISO Z39-48-1992
(Permanence of Paper).

To my revered friends, Dr. Roger Burke and Mrs. Mary Margaret Burke.

Contents

Preface

This book has come into existence with the original idea of writing an extensive commentary on Gaudapādacarya's work, called *Māndūkya Kārikā,* which is highly philosophical, and more advanced psychologically and philosophically than the Western approaches. Very few people know this great scholar and sage in the West. His work is actually a synthesis of the Hindu way of *sādhāna* and the Buddhist way of sādhāna. His independent and highly provocative commentary is worth studying.

Swami Rama comes from the heritage of the great sage and scholar, Shankara, the architect of the *Advaita—* nondual system. In this first volume, only the original Upanishad comprising twelve verses has been explained by him from an experiential standpoint. The second volume, which is in preparation, makes a detailed commentary on the Kārikā. This first volume will be useful for psychologists, therapists, and philosophers, and especially to those aspirants who are aspiring to realize the Ultimate Truth.

Pandit Rajmani Tigunait has assisted Swamiji throughout in writing this book. Dr. Susan Thornburg and Dr. Arpita have devoted long hours in taking down dictation, editing, and making it available for final printing. The final script was reviewed by Dr. Phil Nuernberger and Dr. John Harvey. Barb Bova, a medical student, typed and retyped the original manuscript. Compliments are due to Patrice Hafford for typesetting, Mr. Charles Blanchard for printing, and Randy Padorr-Black for art and design.

Chapter

1

Awakening

Awakening

Rise, awake, and gain knowledge.

—Katha-Up.

    The Vedas are the most ancient scriptures in the library of man today. For ages, their knowledge has been imparted through the oral tradition. No author has ever been attributed to these scriptures. The eternal laws of life and the universe expressed in these scriptures were revealed to seers and sages who devoted their entire lives to the realization of Ultimate Truth. These seers received this knowledge not through sense perception or the mind, but through inner vision directly from the source of intuition during the deepest states of contemplation and meditation. Other levels of knowledge give only a partial glimpse, but intuitive knowledge is self-evident and complete. It is the highest of all knowledge. Such knowledge derived from the center of consciousness through intuition is called *śruti*. *Śruti* means that which is heard by the innermost ear of the sages and seers when in the deepest state of contemplation. It is used to refer to the verses of the Vedas and the Upanishads.

There are two channels of knowledge: direct and indirect. Direct knowledge is transcendent *(parā)*; it is self-evident and experienced from the ultimate source. Indirect knowledge is sensory or mental *(aparā)*; it is knowledge from the external world, or the knowledge gained through waking, dreaming, and deep sleep. It is perceived by the intellect through the senses and mind, and thus is conditioned by time, space, and causation. Direct knowledge is not perceived through the senses and mind because it is the knowledge of Absolute Reality, *turīya*. It is neither object nor subject but is pure experience of the Self by the self. This knowledge is not knowledge through the mind but through vision revealed in the deepest state of realization. Whenever direct knowledge is imparted by an enlightened sage to a student, the student comprehends the knowledge through his intellect. Such knowledge is considered to be indirect knowledge. The only way to attain direct knowledge is through meditation and contemplation, which lead one to the infinite library of eternal wisdom. Transcendental knowledge can be attained only directly from within, and the Upanishads provide methods and means for going to that source. The goal of the Upanishads is to lead the aspirant to the realization of comprehensive knowledge of waking, dreaming, and sleeping and finally to establish him in the fourth state, *turīya*.

The finest section of the Vedas is comprised of the Upanishadic literature, which is generally known as Vedānta. The word *Upanishad* literally means to sit and listen to the preceptor who has attained Brahman-consciousness and who is fully enlightened. The Upanishads are written in Sanskrit language, but knowledge of the language alone is not sufficient for comprehending the knowledge of the Upanishads. The word *Vedānta* literally means the very end or culmination of Vedic knowledge. All the major schools of Indian philosophy and several branches of psychology evolved from this vast storehouse of knowledge. The Upanishads are said to be the epitome of Vedic knowledge and the treasure of the innermost experiences derived by the Vedic sages. There are more than two hundred Upanishads, and, of them, one hundred and eight are available to the common reader. There are many commentaries on the Upanishads, but the most ancient ones available are those of Shankara, the most brilliant Vedantic philosopher and the architect of Advaita philosophy. He chose eleven principal Upanishads for his commentaries, and these Upanishads are considered to be the main source of Vedantic philosophy. Though there are many great religious books in the world, the Upanishadic literature has been a principle source of inspiration for the educated and intellectual person or student, for the Upanishads transcend any particular religious orientation.

The interpretation of the nature and definition of truth, which is still a matter of dispute among modern thinkers, has been thoroughly investigated by the ancient sages. Vedānta philosophy is unique, for it sets before itself the prime questions to be solved, and it also provides a method for finding the Ultimate Truth. This literature unveils all the mysteries of life and logically answers the prime questions that other books leave unanswered. These questions include, "Who am I? From where have I come? Why have I come? Where will I go?" The Upanishads also explain the relationship of the individual to other individuals and creatures of the world, and they finally lead one to understand the status of the individual in the universe. The Upanishads help the human mind to realize the actual unity of consciousness dwelling within the apparent diversity of nature, and they declare that there is only one principle, the Absolute Truth, which is self-existent and not subject to change, death, or decay. One who has realized this truth knows no fear, loves all, and excludes none.

Vedānta philosophy is an *adhyātma-vāda* (that which comes under the domain of Ātman) philosophy in which every sacrifice is made to attain the center of consciousness, and all other duties occupy a minor position. To be an aspirant with the goal of attaining the Truth, one needs to have certain qualifications, the primary being nonattachment, because without it the study of scriptures and practice would be impossible. The student of Vedānta is delighted to renounce all material belongings, relationships, and every feeling and thought of worldly possessions for the sake of attaining the Truth. Complete nonattachment is the first prerequisite for the student of this path. Unless the student's mind is completely purged of all stains and samskāras that cause attachment, one cannot make one's mind one-pointed and inward. According to Vedānta, there are two definite paths.

In one, the aspirant renounces all he has and is attached to, including thoughts, desires, and feelings. This is the path of renunciation, which is meant for a fortunate few;

those who are fully awakened can alone follow this path. In the other path, the aspirant learns to perform his duties without any attachment, renouncing the fruits of his actions so that the actions and the fruits therein do not create any bondage for him. He also can attain the Ultimate Truth. Shankara and other great renunciates believed in renouncing all one's possessions literally, but aspirants like Janaka believed in living in the world yet remaining above. The followers of both paths can attain the fourth state, turīya, the center of Supreme Consciousness.

Only the student of Vedānta understands the necessity of complete, voluntary withdrawal to develop a concentrated mind free from prejudice. No such discipline or requirement has ever been prescribed in other schools of philosophy in either the East or the West. According to this literature, the root cause of all misery is ignorance, which occurs when the ego manifests itself and separates one from the whole. Without totally going beyond the ego, liberation, therefore, is not possible. In order to be aware of the Universal Consciousness, one has to transcend one's own individuality, for it creates the barrier between one and the Universal Consciousness. All personal discoveries and knowledge are transpersonalized when the individual consciousness is expanded into Universal Consciousness.

In order to comprehend the meaning of the Upanishads, one must especially train the mind and its modifications, because only a purified mind is able to comprehend the profound subtle meaning of these scriptures. The meaning of the mantras of the Upanishads lies hidden within the varied frequencies of the vibrations of the most subtle sounds that can be experienced at the deepest levels of consciousness. The grammar used to convey the meanings of these sounds is called *Niruktam,* "that which explains the origin of sounds and their vibrations." The mind of modern man has been trained to look, verify, and judge in the external world, but it has not been trained to look within, find within, and be aware of the inner dimensions of life. Philosophy in the West consists of speculation that uses logic, but Vedānta philosophy is more experiential than speculative, and it is far more advanced than western scientific, psychological, and philosophical thought. Those who have completely devoted their lives to the philosophical pursuit of Truth and who are also thoroughly acquainted with the modern viewpoint can help the contemporary aspirant to study Vedānta.

Māndūkya Upanishad

Māndūkya Upanishad is considered to be more profound than any other Upanishad. It is declared in *Muktika Upanishad that* if one studies and practices the teachings of the *Māndūkya Upanishad,* one acquires the knowledge to attain enlightenment. This Upanishad is not a book of mere mysticism, theology, or scholasticism, but is a sound philosophical scripture. Shankara wrote a commentary on this Upanishad, but the most provocative and brilliant commentary is the *Kārikā* of Gaudapāda, Shankara's teacher's teacher. The Kārikā is an ancient scripture which states that both external and internal experiences are invalid in comparison to the experience of the Ultimate Truth, the very center of consciousness. Very few Westerners know about this Upanishad and the Kārikā, and those who are familiar with them know them only intellectually. But without the practices given in this Upanishad, their real meaning cannot be experienced. The Kārikā commentary is the subject matter of the second volume of this book. This volume explains only the original Māndūkya verses and the way of practice related to them. This volume is written for those students who actually want to practice the method according to this Upanishad, and they will find that the schools of meditation and contemplation, though different, complement one another.

This Upanishad discusses the nature of the material and mental worlds, the nature of consciousness, and the meaning of causality. It accomplishes this by offering an experiential interpretation of the three states of individual self and the state which lies beyond. The three states of individual self are waking *(vaiśvānara),* dreaming *(taijasa),* and deep sleep *(prājña).* The fourth state (turīya) is the state of pure consciousness, which is Absolute Reality— Brahman, Ātman. This Upanishad teaches that awareness of one or more of the first three states is only partial knowledge and can yield only partial truth. Progressively gaining knowledge of more subtle states—their nature, purpose, and functioning in daily life—is the natural process of human growth. But knowledge of Absolute Truth is realized only when one has attained the fourth state, pure consciousness.

This Upanishad describes a framework that the individual can use to reinterpret the data from the first three states and understand the actual underlying truth hidden within the apparent reality. It also describes how the eternal sound Om represents the entire universe, and how Om relates to the four states of consciousness. Three sounds constitute Om, just as various states constitute consciousness *A* is the waking state, *U* is the dreaming state, and *M* is the sleeping state. The fourth state is the silence following the preceding three. Contrary to the dictum of modern linguistics which states that the word is not the thing, the philosophy of sound explained in this Upanishad goes deeper to a more subtle level in which the sound is identical to the object.

The stages of human growth, consciousness, and the eternal sound Om can be clarified by an analogy. The view one can see from the ground floor of a mansion is likened to the experience of the waking state, *A*. The broader perspective of the second story is likened to the experience of the dreaming state, *U*. The more complete vista seen from the third story is likened to the experience of the sleeping state, *M*. But the entire panorama beheld from the roof is like the experience of the fourth state of silence, turīya. From this point of view, one realizes that Om is the entire mansion, whereas the letters *A, U,* and *M* are only the individual stories.

Ordinary human existence is defined by concepts of space, causation, and time with its three conditions, past, present, and future. This structure restricts human experience to the external world and does not encompass the full territory of human existence. But the Māndūkya provides a comprehensive map for the inward journey that shows the individual the way from the mundane to the eternal. It then describes this state, the Ultimate Reality, the goal of human existence.

The whole of Advaita philosophy is encapsulated in these twelve short verses or śrutis. This Upanishad presents the monistic view, Advaita, which is beyond dualism and points out the unity within apparent diversity. A fundamental concept of Tantra philosophy, the relationship of mantra (sound) and yantra (form), is also described in Māndūkya. The profundity of this philosophy is reflected by the fact that it expresses the basis for many other paths and schools of philosophy, including raja yoga, laya yoga, kundalinī yoga, and many of the systems of Indian philosophy and Eastern psychology. This is a practical philosophy that needs to be applied experientially to be known. But intellectual understanding of the concepts expressed in these terse śrutis is the first step to realizing Universal Consciousness.

Philosophy, Not Religion

The Upanishadic literature is not a religious scripture and is free from dogma and doctrines. It is not a part of any religion but is a philosophy for all times and for all. This philosophy does not oppose any school of thought, religion, or interpretation of the scriptures, but its methods for explaining its concepts are unique. The Upanishads should not be confused with the religious books of the East; there is a vast difference between the philosophy of the Upanishads and the preachings of any of the religious scriptures of the world. In religion and religious books, there is little practicality and much theory. One is not supposed to interpret religious sayings, for there is always the possibility of distortion. For this reason, their explanation is delegated to a few teachers and preachers who are considered to be the custodians and authorities on these scriptures. Common people do not have the opportunity to study the scriptures in depth, but instead must rely on the interpretations of such preachers who may show no signs of enlightenment and yet have influence over the conscience of the masses. Whether these clerics actually know and practice religious truths or not is never questioned, and those who do question are considered to be atheists and heretics. Intellectual bankruptcy such as this leads the masses to blind faith and causes many wars and divisions in the human race. For the younger generation today, however, empty religious preachings are not fulfilling, for the modern mind likes to use reason and logic before it accepts anything as truth.

With the development of science and technology, there has arisen a provocative mind that questions the existing religions and their role in society. The modern mind has started questioning, but the search for truth still remains obscured because scientific explorations are directed externally and not toward the inner levels of life. Science and technology are materially oriented, but a human being is not matter or energy alone. Most human resources are currently being directed to matter, mind, and energy, but little effort is being made toward the expansion and exploration of human consciousness. Modern psychologists are scratching the surface of mental life in order to eliminate superficial human problems in the external world, but the vital questions of life are not yet resolved, for they are beyond the grasp of materially-oriented thinking.

The Upanishads prepare, inspire, and lead the student to know and realize the Ultimate Truth. First of all, the philosophy of the Upanishads frees one to cast away his intellectual slavery to blind faith, superstitions, sectarian beliefs, and dogmas. Then it helps one to expand his individual consciousness to Universal Consciousness; thus one's personality is transformed, and one becomes a universal being. An individual is essentially Brahman, or identical to Universal Consciousness, and direct realization of that truth is called enlightenment. Current religious preachings, on the other hand, are enveloped in a thick layer of dust, and they need a complete shakeup. Religion needs modification to suit the needs of modern man. There seem to be two options for humanity: either it stops listening to the preachings, starts seeking the truth, and rejoices in the broader awareness of truthful living; or it continues to follow religious dogma, fails to attain the next step of civilization, and remains in ignorance and suffering. Upon careful analysis of the living and thinking structure of modern human society, anyone can see that the process of human evolution is in a state of stagnation. All current research is directed to the external world; thus the human goal has become materially oriented and superficial. Human beings today have nothing better to live for than acquiring many comforts. These may be necessities and means, but because attaining them lacks a goal or aim, they create a hollow and empty philosophy that brings only strain and stress.

The preachings of religion make a person dependent on priests, temples, idols, blind faith, and dogma, and dependence is a habit of the lower mind. Such crutches may be useful at a certain stage for some people, but they do not lead one to Ultimate Truth. A dependent mind is not free, and without freedom, enlightenment is impossible. Religious dogmas are full of beliefs and myths that do not satisfy the human intellect and that bind believers to a narrow view of life and human potential. Such preachings instill more fear than love in the hearts of the masses. Religion either promises salvation or threatens the tortures of hell, but it does not provide sound solutions to the hellish problems and situations that plague human beings here and now.

Nor does it satisfactorily explain life before birth or after death. One of the main themes of Upanishadic philosophy, however, is to attain a state of fearlessness, cheerfulness, and self-confidence. In addition, the Upanishads lead the student to know life in its totality. Knowledge of life before birth, knowledge of now, and knowledge of life hereafter can be realized through the methods given in the Upanishads. The Upanishads provide systematic methods for self-training, self-transformation, and self-enlightenment. They lead aspirants "from the unreal to the Real, from darkness to Light, and from mortality to Immortality."

The founders of religion were selfless and sincere— great seers, sages, and spiritual leaders. But as religions grew, the teachings of the founders were lost, and only the preachings of their selfish followers remained. Because of this, the great religion of the East was reduced to the narrow faith and beliefs of Hinduism, Brahmanism, Buddhism, and Jainism. Practical Christianity also disappeared forever, and there remained only churchianity. History shows that religionists do not actually encourage one to follow in the footsteps of the founder of their religion by practicing his teachings, but, rather, they instruct their followers to worship the image or the name of the founder of the religion through priests. Many religious leaders who claim to know God are more miserable than those they attempt to lead; they suffer from trite egoism, jealousy, and selfishness. The light of truth cannot shine through such barriers. Thus, the blind are leading the blind. The philosophy of the Upanishads is not bound by a single founder or religion, however, and it is as applicable today as it was thousands of years ago, and it will be so for as long as humanity exists.

Religious dogma sets forth rigid commandments presented in terms of good and bad, black and white, with no explanations to support them. In the long run, these create serious overreactions and overcompensations in the human mind. All the books from the different religions repeat set laws of conduct in the same way, yet each of these religions claims that it is superior to all the others. Religious beliefs may offer solace to lower, primitive, less educated, and uncultivated minds, but they have nothing to offer those who already know what to do and what not to do, and who are seeking logical solutions to life's questions and guidance in learning how to be. In today's so-called civilized society, the moral laws preached by the leaders and preachers seem to be incomplete. Such teachings and preachings are, therefore, misleading and are a mere waste of time and energy. As long as the preachers, police, and army have to guard the morality of human beings, this cannot be considered to be a civilized society. The moral custodians of today's world are actually atomic weapons, not the laws given in the religious books of the world. Thus, material forces are guiding the destiny of human life. Human beings have lost their center of equilibrium and live without any sense of equality, love, and mutual understanding. Religions do not teach unity but create divisions in human society. The Upanishads do not impose commandments, but, rather, offer practical guidelines and methods for self-discipline and self-unfoldment. The steps for inner growth contained in the Upanishads can be incorporated into one's individual lifestyle and can help one examine the accomplishments of one's spiritual practice (sādhāna).

Religions can be divided into two groups. One group follows the prophets but does not believe in inner experience. These religions are actually cults and are full of rituals, fear, guilt, and fanaticism. The other group of religions has a vast spiritual literature, but the followers are exploited by priests who involve them in rituals without explaining their purpose or establishing their validity. Therefore, both types of religion have been exploiting humanity and, thus, crippling human efforts to evolve and attain the next step of civilization in which people will learn to live with others in mutual understanding and love. The vast majority of the human population practices religious rituals in some way or other, but no ritual exists that can eliminate the ignorance that causes pain and misery.

Religions have two great weapons to conquer the hearts of their followers: faith and grace. The way faith is described in religious scriptures is not actually faith at all, but is blind belief based on ignorance and rigidity of tradition. Tradition and truth are entirely different. One is mingled with customs, systems, cultures, habits, thoughts, feelings, and desires, and the latter is a search for the Ultimate Reality. For attaining truth, everything the aspirant has, including thoughts, deeds, and speech, becomes a means for attaining truth; while in tradition, all means are used for the sake of convenience, pleasure, and gratification. Religionists and their faithful followers are afraid to analyze the very nature of their faith. Thus, one is lost in a morass of religious fanaticism. Faith that does not recognize the faculty of reasoning and that has not been filtered by reasoning is based on blind beliefs that remain unexamined. They thus unnecessarily create doubts, and when doubts are not resolved, such faith disappears. Blind faith, being empty and devoid of any real reason or fact, is often found wanting when one has a problem and expects to find a strong basis that will support and carry him through difficult times. Then one finds, instead, nothing to hold on to or anchor oneself to. Because of this weakness in religious faith, religious dogma says that faith is a gift from God, and that if one questions it, then it might vanish and be lost. True faith is supported by pure reason, which is attained through thoughtful analysis of life. Following the extended practice of sādhāna and purification, a few fortunate seekers realize and know the nature of the world as it is and also experience the all-pervading truth that enlightens the dark chamber of the aspirant's heart.

The Upanishads say that to rise above and reach a state beyond and to know the real nature of the transitory world, one must cultivate logic and pure reason and make sincere efforts with the help of deep contemplation. They declare, "Only that which is good and auspicious in Upanishadic literature should be revered and brought into practice, and the rest should be left behind for further introspection."

In religions, grace is considered to be a gift bestowed on the seeker, either as a reward for following the commandments or by mere whim. Thus, the bestowing of blessings serves as a bribe to make one conform, and it implies that the seeker is helpless to succeed by his own effort. There is often little sense of individual mastery but rather a reliance on the favors of fate or the judgments of the preachers. Fear and insecurity are the logical results.

Today religion has degenerated so much that it has become totally materialistic. No matter how good a heart one has, if one is not on the list of followers and supporters of the church, then one's faith does not have any value in the eyes of religionists. Religious leaders and preachers who claim to be custodians of faith and grace sell faith to blind followers for wealth and favors, and, thus, religious materialism takes the place of spiritual sincerity. Various schools of theology argue over the semantics and meaning of the verses and parables of religious scriptures and never reach any shared interpretation. In order to confront the question of life, one must remain unaffected by religious dogma, doctrines, and superstition, and one must make use of one's finest instrument, the intellect. The Upanishads do not encourage students to depend on the sayings of the scriptures; rather they inspire them to be self-reliant and discriminating. Religious dogma encourages people to follow the canons of a particular sectarian belief that is limited to a specific group. Thus, instead of expanding universal brotherhood, it further divides humanity and pollutes human feelings with biases and prejudice. Upanishadic philosophy is the expression of supreme knowledge directly experienced by great sages and is not confined to caste, color, society, or nation.

Today the world lives under the law of fear, trembling with doubts and uncertainty. No prophet of the law of love is to be found, and one finds no leaders who give object lessons, sympathy, and good will, and who identify with the true happiness of individuals and nations and the highest good of mankind. Many religious leaders exist, but it is amazing to note how tired and confused they are. "Rise, awake, and gain knowledge"— this Upanishad declares that one should not act like a gigantic inert person who is dumb and desolate, who knows not the meaning of life and the universe. All human beings have the essential potentialities to understand and direct their life streams toward the ocean of bliss. The message of Upanishadic philosophy extends good will to the whole of humanity, saying, "Let all of mankind be happy; let all of humanity attain physical, mental, and spiritual health; let all receive and enjoy auspiciousness; let no one experience pain and misery here and hereafter."

What God Is

All the religions of the world have been promising the vision of God, mental peace, salvation, and many kinds of temptations to their followers, but so far nothing has come true. The more that people are involved in sectarian religious activities, the more likely they are to become disappointed because of frustrated expectations of God and religion. Many preachers claim that if their teachings are followed without question, believers will find salvation. But after they return from their church or temple, they are frequently more stressed, frustrated, and worried about their problems than are "non-believers."

Mere belief in God alone does not satisfy the students of life who are searching for Ultimate Truth. Suppose a student believes in the existence of God but is not emotionally mature and does not have a peaceful mind. Such a student does not have tranquility and equanimity, which are the main prerequisites for enlightenment. On the path of enlightenment, it is necessary to have control over the senses and mind, but it is not necessary to have belief in God. Enlightenment is a state of freedom from the ignorance that causes suffering, and attaining this is the prime necessity of every human life. There is no necessity to attain mere belief in God, but it is necessary to have profound knowledge of the truth which lies behind the concept of the word *God*.

The word *G-O-D* is not God. The religionists, because they superimpose their own limited fantasies upon the truth and call it God, suffer more than the people who do not believe in the concept of God. If Ultimate Truth is called God, then there is no difficulty. Then it can be practiced with mind, action, and speech, and once the truth is known with mind, action, and speech, knowledge is complete. But having faith in the fantasies of the religionists creates limited boundaries for the human intellect and leads to a religious atmosphere in which the poor followers must suffer until the last breaths of their lives.

Though religious dogma tempts the human mind with promises of the vision of God, it does not clarify and define the concept of God. The way religious books present the picture of God is injurious to human growth, for one who believes in God without understanding what God really is, closes the door to further knowledge and learning and cannot experience the inner dimensions of life. Such false promises are strongly discouraged in the Upanishads, which warn, "*Neti, neti*—not this, not this." The student is made aware of the need to understand the reality and is encouraged to search for truth within. The Upanishads inspire one first to know oneself and then to know the Self of all. Upanishadic literature makes one aware that every being embodied in a physical sheath is a moving shrine of Supreme Consciousness. It also provides methods for entering the inner shrine, wherein shines the infinite light of knowledge, peace, and happiness.

Prayer is a major technique used by religionists to seek satisfaction of their desires and comfort in spite of their frustrations. Many people who are not acquainted with the basic principles of Vedantic philosophy think that there are prayers in the Upanishadic literature. For example: "Lead me from the unreal to the Real; lead me from darkness to Light; lead me from mortality to Immortality" may be thought to be a prayer. But it is actually an expression of the aspirant's spiritual desires that remind him of his goal of life constantly. It is not a prayer but a way of maintaining constant awareness of Supreme Consciousness. It is not asking God or any supernatural being to help one or to lead one to the higher states. The idea is not to know God as a different being, but to know one's own real Self and its essential nature, which is the Self of all. One is not attaining something that is not already there but is realizing that which is self-existent. This Upanishadic verse is not a prayer asking for anything but a way of strengthening constant awareness of Supreme Consciousness which is the goal of the Upanishads.

Dualism is the preliminary experience of a contemplative mind. All religions suffer on account of dualistic concepts, such as "Human beings are a creation of God; the universe is a creation of God; human beings have no choice but to suffer and should delight in their sufferings at the mercy of God." These concepts are illogical when they are analyzed with clarity of mind and pure reason. In the course of study, a student first experiences dualism—the reality that he exists and the Supreme Consciousness also exists. Then a state comes when he experiences "Thou art That." These two fields of experience appear to be different, but they are essentially one and the same. These are the progressive states that aspirants experience, but as far as Absolute Reality is concerned, there is only one without second.

Religionists say the ultimate goal of human life is to

know God, and materialists say it is to eat, drink, and be merry. But the philosophy of the Upanishads asserts that the ultimate goal is to be free from all pain and misery whatsoever. This state of freedom from anxieties, misery, and ignorance is called enlightenment. It is the union of the individual with Universal Consciousness. Religionists say that one has to have faith in the sayings of the scriptures and in the way they are preached. But in Upanishadic philosophy, the mind is released from all religious prejudices so then one can think and reason freely. The Upanishads declare that even the best of intellects is incapable of fathoming the unfathomable, and that learning the scriptures is not the ultimate way of realization. On the path of enlightenment, even the lust for learning must eventually be abandoned.

In some of the Upanishads, the word *Īśa* or *Īśvara,* which is roughly translated as God, appears. But the concept of God as preached by religion is not found in the Upanishads. In the Upanishads, the word *Īśvara* is used to denote a state of collective consciousness. Thus, God is not a being that sits on a high pedestal beyond the sun, moon, and stars; God is actually the state of Ultimate Reality. But due to the lack of direct experience, God has been personified and given various names and forms by religions throughout the ages. When one expands one's individual consciousness to the Universal Consciousness, it is called Self-realization, for the individual self has realized the unity of diversity, the very underlying principle, or Universal Self, beneath all forms and names. The great sages of the Upanishads avoid the confusions related to conceptions of God and encourage students to be honest and sincere in their quests for Self-realization. Upanishadic philosophy provides various methods for unfolding higher levels of truth and helps students to be able to unravel the mysteries of the individual and the universe.

Knowledge of *Brahmavidyā,* the direct experience of Supreme Consciousness, is the common theme of all Upanishadic literature. "I am Brahman; the whole universe is Brahman; Thou art That"—such statements are the foundations for all its theories, principles, and practices. All philosophical and psychological discussions are meant to make students aware of their true nature—Brahman, the Supreme Consciousness. For a realized one, there is perennial joy in the universe, but for the ignorant there is only misery everywhere. The moment a student realizes his essential nature, the darkness of ignorance is dispelled, but before that the individual mind travels to the groove of self-created misery and thus projects the belief that there is misery everywhere. In reality, this universe is like a great poem of joy, a beautiful song, and a unique work of art. The moment one unfolds and realizes one's human capacity and ability, one becomes aware that, "Thou art that—Brahman."

Here lies the difference between a Self-realized person and a religionist. The religionist does not know and yet believes in God, but the realized person is directly aware of the self-existent Ultimate Reality of life and the universe. First, he knows the truth, and then he believes it. If God is the Ultimate Truth hidden behind many forms and names, then it should be realized, and, for realizing the Truth with mind, action, and speech, one needs to practice truth rather than being a hypocrite and a fanatic. It is not necessary to believe in God to attain self-enlightenment, but it is very necessary to know the various levels of consciousness and finally to realize the ultimate source. The manifest aspect and the unmanifest aspect of consciousness (Brahman) should be realized, for that alone can enlighten aspirants.

What is Brahman?

The word *Brahman* is derived from the Sanskrit verb root *brha* or *brhi,* meaning expansion, knowledge, or all-pervasiveness. This word is always of a neuter gender; it indicates Absolute Reality beyond the concept of male and female and all other dualities. Brahman is omnipresent, omniscient, omnipotent; it is the very nature of one's true Self. That Absolute Reality, that Supreme Consciousness, which is never affected by the ever-changing nature of the world, is Brahman. That which alone exists and allows the entire universe to appear within itself is called Brahman. That Brahman is no different from oneself; all of humanity is Brahman. From this point of view, all people are essentially one and the same. Placing duality and diversity within humanity is the greatest loss, and realizing the oneness within and without is the highest gain.

Universality and the State Beyond

Attaining knowledge of Brahman directly from within is called enlightenment. The human mind is in the habit of experiencing and projecting pains and pleasures, but when it is made aware of the everlasting Truth, one starts seeing things as they are. The mind identifies itself with the objects of the external world and thus places a veil between the aspirant and the Reality, but the moment this self-created veil of māyā (illusion) is removed, one attains freedom. The

veil of ignorance covers human consciousness on three
levels: the states of waking, dreaming, and deep sleep.
Unless the veil over all these levels is lifted, the light of pure
consciousness cannot shine. Thus, permeating one's consciousness to the state beyond and expanding it to the
Supreme Consciousness is called enlightenment. From the
heights of enlightenment, one remains aware of all states—
waking, dreaming, and deep sleep—and yet remains in the
state beyond—turīya. Before casting off his body, such an
enlightened sage lives in the world yet remains above. He
sees himself in the whole cosmos and the whole cosmos in
himself. His self becomes the Self of all.

This direct experience of the oneness of all, of loving
all and excluding none, is called *Brahma-vihāra*—frolicking
in Brahman. This realization cannot be attained through
mere reasoning or through the intellect; nor can it be
attained through mere study of the scriptures, listening to
teachers, or repeating prayers without feeling all day long.
The Upanishads say that only that fortunate one to whom
the knowledge of the Self is revealed can experience the joy
and bliss of enlightenment. Unless a student opens the
petals of the heart, knowledge of the divine experience is
never revealed. Sincere effort with perfect surrender to the
Absolute Reality alone is the way to welcome the dawn of
eternal knowledge and peace.

The Upanishads are not religious scriptures, but they
can provide the foundation for universality through the
practical philosophy of equality, equanimity, love, and
universal brotherhood. Modern man is trying to improve
the quality of life and achieve the next step of civilization.
But without utilizing the concepts explained in the teachings
of Upanishadic philosophy, it is impossible to resolve the

bitterness of black and white discrimination, male and female chauvinism, ethnocentric egoism, or intellectual slavery to religious dogma and superstitions. Unless all people extend their hands to help one another, to share with all, and to communicate with all, humanity cannot be called a civilized species. When humanity follows that universality based on the Upanishadic philosophy, there will be no need for discipline enforced by the state, for codes of conduct, or for courts and churches. People will be self-disciplined and will progress constantly towards self-enlightenment.

Humanity has to expand the philosophy of life to enable it to rise above the narrow confines of religion, creed, and ethnic identification. To attain the next step, one has to become a member of the universal family and a worshipper of the Supreme Reality. When one understands the teachings of the Upanishads, then one realizes that life itself is a sort of worship that can shine on the altar of infinity. The hearts of all individuals should beat in one rhythm; the music of the pulse should resonate to a single melody. The time of practicing and following universality will come, and the flower of humanity will blossom. Then the humanity will share all material things as it shares the sun, air, and rain. This can be done when people determine to enlighten themselves, and enlightenment is possible here and now without the help of the word *God*.

Chapter
2

Māṇḍūkya
Upanishad

हरिः ॐ। ओमित्येतदक्षरमिदं सर्वं तस्योपव्याख्यानं भूतं भवद्भविष्यदिति सर्वमोंकार एव। यच्चान्यत् त्रिकालातीतं तदप्योंकार एव।।१।।

Hariḥ Om. Om-ity-etad-akṣaram-idaṁ sarvaṁ tasyopavyākhyānaṁ bhūtaṁ bhavad bhaviṣyad-iti sarvam-omkāra eva. Yaccānyat trikālātītaṁ tad apy omkāra eva.

Hari Om. The entire universe is the syllable Om. The following is the exposition of Om. Everything in the past, present, and future is verily Om. That which is beyond time, space, and causation is also Om.

All this is Om. All manifested objects of the world and all unmanifested states of reality are denoted by this syllable Om. Om is the imperishable, eternal sound. Om is also the name of the Absolute Reality, both manifest and unmanifest. Om is the Reality on all dimensions, and the Reality is Om. The aspect of Reality that manifested in the past, remains manifest in the present, and will manifest in the future, is Om. The Absolute Reality that is not conditioned by the past, present, and future is also Om. If Om is a word, the whole universe is its explanation. If it is a sound, the whole universe is its vibration. If it is representative, it represents both the manifested and unmanifested aspects of the cosmos.

Om is the syllable and sound that represents all levels of consciousness. All potentialities, forms, and thoughts are expressions of Om, the infinite and unmanifest power that is not subject to change. All expressions are manifested by and finally return to their original unmanifested source, Om. All other words have been derived from this eternal word, which is the name of the Absolute Reality. Om is the eternal source of speech *(vāk)*. All phenomena and all desires emanate from that infinite source, Om. The fulfillment of all desires depends upon knowledge of it, and one's desires are fulfilled in proportion to one's progress towards it. Worldly pleasures are transient, but the truth reveals eternal wisdom and bliss. Om is the eternal sound that expands the individual consciousness to Universal Consciousness. The aspirant who meditates on Om and contemplates on its meaning understands the Absolute Truth.

Om is a syllable, a symbol, and a sound that does not belong to any particular language. When one studies the symbol, the syllable, and the sound individually and collectively, one receives the knowledge of all the levels of reality—gross, subtle, subtlemost, and beyond. All desires, thoughts, and feelings cannot be brought into action and expressed through speech because the senses, through which one expresses oneself, do not have that capacity. The language used in daily life for learning, communicating, and knowing is so shallow that the vast bulk of knowledge remains buried in the supreme library of the unconscious, and only a very little part of it can be expressed. One's desires, thoughts, and feelings, therefore, mostly remain untranslated, and the more one learns of the reality of inner levels, the more one finds difficulty in the limitations of human language. Sages often used symbols, such as Om, and interpreted them to make their students aware of an aspect of knowledge that could not be expressed by language. All the symbols that travel in the mental train during the dream state and meditation are not meaningless; they have definite content, and they are translated according to the context and nature of the dream. The special method used to know a symbol is the knowledge of the sounds that vibrate to form the symbol. Suppose one makes a sound by clapping two hands—that sound will vibrate and create a particular form. By studying the form one can study the quality and intensity of the sound and its vibrations, and by studying the sound, one can also come to know the form. The entire Upanishadic teachings are condensed in the knowledge of Om. One who knows Om in theory and practice knows everything about life, the universe, and Absolute Truth.

The teachings of the Upanishads are higher than those of other scriptures. The words of the seers are meaningful and applicable and are full of knowledge and wisdom, for they originate at the deepest level of consciousness. But the knowledge that comes through the intellect and mind in an academic and scholastic way is inferior to the knowledge received by the sages in deep contemplation and meditation.

The sayings of the sages leave a profound impact on the hearts and minds of aspirants, while the knowledge derived through the intellect is incomplete and has no lasting effect.

2

सर्वं ह्येतद् ब्रह्मायमात्मा ब्रह्म सोयमात्मा चतुष्पात् ।।२।।

Sarvaṁ hy-etad brahmāyam-ātmā brahma so'yam- ātmā catuṣpāt.

All this, whatsoever is seen here, there, and everywhere, is Brahman. This very Self, Ātman, is Brahman, the Absolute Reality. This Ātman has four aspects.

All that is is Brahman, the Supreme Consciousness. The essential nature of the individual self (Ātman) is Brahman, the Universal Self—I am That. That Self is experienced on four levels, and so consciousness is considered to have four states. Three of the states are those experienced during waking, dreaming, and deep sleep, and the fourth is a state beyond. Consciousness experienced in the first three states is called Apara-Brahman, and consciousness experienced in the fourth state is called Para-Brahman. Vaiśvānara, taijasa, and prājña are the states of consciousness—waking, dreaming, and sleeping—and the fourth state is the supreme one, called turīya. The experience of waking merges into dreaming, dreaming merges into deep sleep, and ultimately deep sleep merges into turīya. Thus, turīya encompasses all the other states.

In the Upanishads, Om is the representative name and symbol of Brahman. For the sake of sādhāna, it is the designator of Absolute Reality, and by meditating upon it, one realizes the Ultimate Truth. Ātman, the individual self, and Brahman, the Universal Self, are one and the same. When the student realizes that Universal Consciousness is all-pervading, then he also realizes that Ātman and Brahman are not two separate identities with two different existences. He realizes that they are one, "Thou art That." When the individual self realizes that it is essentially Brahman, it gets freedom from the bondage of the vehicle called the unconscious mind.

For the sake of analysis, there are three parts: the mortal part—body, senses, breath, and conscious mind; the semi-immortal part—the unconscious mind and the individual self *(jivātman),* and the immortal part—the Self (Ātman). After death, there still exists the unconscious mind, which is the storehouse of merits and demerits, feelings, thoughts, desires, and memories. The unconscious mind is used as a vehicle for the individual self, but when the individual self drops all attachments to the unconscious mind, the individual self establishes itself in its essential nature and realizes that its self is the Self of all. Such a state of realization is called liberation, turīya, the very origin of pure consciousness. The three states of consciousness other than turīya are actually that which is experienced by the individual self on three levels.

The realization of the oneness of Atman and Brahman removes ignorance, or māyā—that which does not exist but seems to be existent. Māyā has no existence of its own, just as darkness has no existence. For lack of light, one experiences darkness, and for lack of knowledge, one remains ignorant. When an aspirant removes the veils of ignorance by being aware of the higher dimensions of consciousness, then he understands that the universe is a grand illusion and that reality is the fourth state, turīya. When the light of knowledge dawns and the aspirant attains the fourth state, he realizes that the individual Ātman and the Universal Brahman are one and the same. But as long as the aspirant's mind experiences only three states of consciousness, he dwells in duality and cannot realize the oneness of Ātman and Brahman. Uninterrupted meditation and constant contemplation lead the student to realize turīya, that Absolute Reality which is self-existent.

This scripture systematically explains three levels of consciousness: waking, dreaming, and sleeping. When the experiencer realizes that the dreaming reality is subtler than the waking reality and that the sleeping reality is deeper than the dreaming reality, he then wants to comprehend collectively the experience of all three realities by attaining Absolute Reality, the fourth state, turīya.

३

जागरितस्थानो बहिष्प्रज्ञः सप्तांग एकोनविंशतिमुरवः स्थूलभुग्वै
श्वानरः प्रथमः पादः ।।३।।

*Jāgarita-sthāno bahiṣ-prajñaḥ saptāṅga ekonaviṃśati-
mukhaḥ sthūla-bhūg vaiśvānaraḥ prathamaḥ pādaḥ.*

The first aspect is the waking state, vaiśvānara. In this state,
consciousness is turned to the external. With its seven
instruments and nineteen channels, it experiences the gross
phenomenal world.

Consciousness in the waking state (vaiśvānara) experiences the objects of the external world. This is the state of consciousness that identifies itself with the physical and pranic sheaths. Its seven instruments are the five elements (earth, water, fire, air, and ether) the breath, and the ego, which identifies itself with the body. Its nineteen channels are the five active senses (speaking, grasping, walking, reproducing, and excreting); the five cognitive senses (hearing, touching, seeing, tasting, and smelling); the five prānas *(prāna, apāna, samāna, udāna,* and *vyāna);* and the four *antahkaranas* or inner instruments (mind, ego, intellect, and *chitta*—the storehouse of memories).

In modern psychology, the dreaming and sleeping states are thought to be unconscious states, but Vedānta psychology explains that they are not actually unconscious for the yogis who can attain conscious access to the dreaming and sleeping states.

Waking is that state of mind in which one remains aware of one's activities in the external environment and of the objects of the world. The waking state is the state of subject / object consciousness. This mode of consciousness is dualistic—one experiences oneself as subject and everything else as object. In waking consciousness, the ego, one of the modifications of the mind, experiences itself as the subject, who is conscious. Thus, it is brought into self-definition and stands out as the figure, while objects remain as the ground. The emergence of the ego as a small island upon which to stand is an important step in the evolution of self-consciousness. The ego enables one to be conscious of oneself, but the self that one is conscious of is extremely circumscribed. One experiences a boundary around oneself, a split from the objects one experiences This leads to a sense of separation or a feeling of alienation from others or from one's environment.

In the waking state of consciousness, one processes experiences in a way that psychoanalysts have termed secondary process functioning. Here the vast majority of information coming from the external environment and from one's memory is filtered by the ego. Thus, much information may be ignored because of the ego's narrow focus on its own particular identification and preoccupations. Waking consciousness is further constricted by the framework of time, space, and causation. In this mode of consciousness, only a portion of one's potential is available to conscious experience and use.

It is important to note that the waking reality alone does not help to unfold the human consciousness. When the reality of the dreaming state is understood thoroughly, one realizes that the dreaming state is more subtle than the waking state. Today, psychologists are trying to analyze and understand the dreaming state from a therapeutic viewpoint. But when one explores the dreaming state through direct experience by using a conscious method of meditation, one can understand the reality of the dreaming state in a comprehensive way. The dreaming state can expand the aspirant's field of knowledge if he knows how to witness the dream. At the same time, he can watch all the symbols, ideas, fancies, fantasies, impressions, memories, repressions, and suppressions coming from the storehouse of the unconscious mind. By understanding the dreaming reality, one can understand the waking reality also. If one has not seen, heard, imagined, thought of, or read something, he cannot dream of it. In the waking state, one cannot go beyond the sphere of knowledge gained during waking.

So analyzing the dreaming state means understanding the waking state also. But by understanding the waking state alone, one cannot understand the dreaming state.

स्वप्नस्थानोन्तःप्रज्ञस्सप्तांग एकोनविंशतिमुरवः प्रविविक्त-
भुक्तैजसो द्वितीयः पादः ।।४।।

Svapna-sthāno 'ntaḥ-prajñaḥ saptāṅga ekonaviṁśati-
mukhaḥ pra-vivikta-bhuk taijaso dvitīyaḥ pādaḥ.

The second aspect is the dreaming state, taijasa. In this state,
consciousness is turned inward. It also has seven instruments and nineteen channels, which experience the subtle
mental impressions.

In the dreaming state (taijasa), the mind is inwardly aware and recalls the subtle impressions of previous experiences stored in the unconscious mind. The dreaming state of consciousness is also said to have seven instruments and nineteen channels because in dreaming, the mind creates the objects of enjoyment as they are found in the external world, and it enjoys them as if it were in the waking state. In dreams, the mind tries to create all the objects that it could not enjoy during wakefulness, and thus it tries to satisfy suppressed and unfulfilled desires. Under the influence of ignorance and desire, this state is experienced as if it were real.

During the waking state, the mind uses the senses for experiencing the objects of the world and employs them for interpreting different types of objects. But in the dreaming state, the mind has withdrawn itself from the senses, and so the flow of impressions stored in the unconscious mind during the waking state comes forward. The dreamer dreams for a reason: there are still desires to be fulfilled. When the body and conscious mind take rest, suddenly impressions hidden in the unconscious come forward from the storehouse of merits, demerits, and memories, in want of fulfilling these desires. So the mind creates an image of the object to fulfill that desire. This is the nature, the functioning, the beauty, of how a human being is structured. If one cannot fulfill a desire in the waking reality, dreams fulfill it in the dreaming reality.

In the waking state, one pushes back all his unfulfilled desires and keeps them pending. Just as one piles papers on his desk, desires are piled up in one's unconscious, and so during dreaming, they all come forward. Then, just as one's secretary brings all the piles of paper and one disposes of them, likewise any desire that is left behind unfulfilled is fulfilled during the dreaming state. Desires that are not fulfilled in the waking state are fulfilled in the dreaming state. But the dreamer is still not satisfied when he awakens, because when he comes back to the reality of the waking state, he forgets the reality of the dreaming state. If the dreamer remains in the dreaming state, he can fulfill all his desires by himself. If the dreamer wants something, it is there with him; his desires can create all the things that he needs. The difference is that in the waking state one employs the senses to collect data from the external world, but in dreaming one recalls the experiences of the past.

Thought patterns, desires, and feelings that want to be satisfied in the external world but are not, are expressed in the dreaming state. This is considered to be therapeutic, and throughout history, the dreaming state has therefore been regarded as a useful mode of consciousness. Although dreams may not be important in themselves, they are useful as a means for providing information to waking consciousness. Since waking consciousness filters out a great deal of useful information that comes through the senses, memory, and extrasensory perception, dreams have been used by the waking consciousness to gain access to some of this information.

In the dreaming state, one processes experiences in a way that psychoanalysts have termed primary process functioning. Here, symbols are used to express multifaceted aspects of experience, and consciousness is not limited by time, space, and causation. In the dreaming state, causal and temporal logic is replaced by symbolic expression.

Dreaming consciousness is complementary to waking consciousness, but generally many people have not established any link between the waking and dreaming states. Though modern science has shown that almost everyone dreams several times each night, many people are not aware of having had any dreams when they awaken. They are like dual personalities, living one existence during the day and another at night, with the two remaining largely unknown to each other. There are various ways to make connections between these two modes of consciousness. Some people have partially integrated the two states by remembering or analyzing aspects of their dreams in the waking state and by bringing their self-awareness and self-regulation into the dreaming state.

5

यत्र सुप्तो न कंचन कामं कामयते न कंचन स्वप्नं पश्यति तत् सुषुप्तम्।
सुषुप्तस्थान एकीभूतः प्रज्ञानघन एवानन्दमयो ह्यानन्दभुक् चेतोमुरवः
प्राज्ञस्तृतीयः पादः ।। ५ ।।

Yatra supto na kañcana kāmaṁ kāmayate na kañcana
svapnaṁ paśyati tat suṣuptam. Suṣupta-sthāna eki-bhūtaḥ
Prajñāna-ghana evānandamayo hy-ānanda-bhuk cheto-
mukhaḥ prājnas tṛtiyaḥ pādaḥ.

The third aspect is deep sleep, prājña. In this state, there is
neither desire nor dream. In deep sleep, all experiences merge
into the unity of undifferentiated consciousness. The sleeper is
filled with bliss and experiences bliss and can find the way
to knowledge of the two preceding states.

Among all three states, waking, dreaming, and sleeping, the sleeping state is the finest. In this state, one experiences the void or deep sleep. This is the unconscious state. When a yogi is able to bring consciousness of the preceding two states to deep sleep, such a state is called prājña. The experience of sleep is different from the sleeping state. In this state, the mind is aware of neither physical nor mental phenomena. In this state, one does not desire, dream of, nor experience material objects, and the conscious mind is withdrawn from the phenomenal world. This state is also a gateway that leads to the experience and understanding of dreaming and wakefulness. As one moves from the waking reality to the dreaming reality to the reality of dreamless sleep, there is a progressive movement away from involvement in the world of objects. To the waking consciousness, the state of dreamless sleep appears to be a state of consciousness of a very high order. Here one experiences unity, in contrast to the diversity of the objects experienced in the waking state. Yogis describe this as a void or a state of purely subjective consciousness that has a blissful quality.

The sleeper ordinarily enters this blissful state a few times each night and replenishes oneself, but unfortunately, one is not able to be consciously aware of being in that state, so one does not fully experience its blissful quality. Yogis, therefore, practice methods for extending self-consciousness into this state. They state that the task of the human being is to become consciously aware of the state of deep sleep, which is the unifier of all manifest states and experiences. But unless the conscious mind is trained to do so, it cannot recall in the waking state memories from the experiences of deep sleep. For the student to progress beyond the three manifest states of consciousness, he must learn to consciously gain access to all those states at will and to realize all three states simultaneously, as well as their unity within himself and the universe. To accomplish this, yogis learn to go into a deep state of voluntary sleep, called *yoga-nidrā,* and yet remain fully aware of the environment. In this state, the clarity of mind is more profound than in the waking state. Often, due to lack of coordination, the mind is clouded and does not remain fully attentive, but in the state of yogic sleep, the mind remains one-pointed and clear. During normal sleep, the sleeper remains close to the Absolute Reality, but he is unaware of the Reality. But this is not the case with meditators.

Those who have attained the state of equilibrium in the fourth state, turīya, consider and can compare death with the sleeping state. Suppose someone manages to live for a hundred years and sleeps eight hours every night. When all the hours he has slept are calculated, one can see that he has slept thirty-three and a third years. Suppose someone sleeps for thirty-three and a third years without interruption. How would he think, remember, and act? Will he recognize his associates, colleagues, and relatives and the things he owned in the same way he remembers these after eight hours of sleep? It is not possible. So sleep can be compared with death, which is a deep sleep for thousands of hours, days, and years in which one sheds one's external garments—body, breath, and conscious mind. After sleep, the sleeper wakes up, and in the same way, after the long sleep of death, one wakes up and assumes new garments. One who knows this reality does not fear death.

This Upanishad refers to deep sleep, prājña, as being

restful, joyous, and blissful, and this bliss-like state is superior to the waking and dreaming states. It is impossible to experience the waking and dreaming states without experiencing the sleeping state. As one cultivates the waking reality and utilizes the flow of consciousness in it, he becomes successful in the world. Similarly, if one understands the dreaming reality and sleeping reality and the consciousness that functions within those different modes of reality, he can enjoy life more than others do. But the highest joy and perennial happiness is realized when one attains the state beyond, turīya. During deep sleep, the joy or bliss that is experienced is definitely higher than the joy attained during the waking and dreaming states, but it is still a pseudoblissful state as compared to the state of turīya.

एष सर्वेश्वर एष सर्वज्ञ एषोऽन्तर्याम्येष योनिः सर्वस्य प्रभवाप्ययौ हि
भूतानाम्।।६।।

*Eṣa sarveśvara eṣa sarva-jña eṣo'ntaryāmy-eṣa yoniḥ
sarvasya prabhavāpyayau hi bhūtānam.*

The experiencer of these states of consciousness is the Lord
of all. This one is all-knowing; this one directs everything
from within. This one is the womb of all. All things originate
from and dissolve into this.

When in meditation and contemplation the aspirant experiences gradual and progressive steps of unfoldment through the waking, dreaming, and sleeping realities, he comes to know that he has not unfolded himself to that extent from which he can comprehend the knowledge of these three states collectively. To attain the collective knowledge of all these states, he attains a higher level, exactly as a mountain climber, who, when he climbs to the top of the mountain, can have comprehensive vision of that which is up above, down below, and behind the mountain. After attaining turīya or the fourth state of consciousness, the aspirant can witness the three states of consciousness separately and collectively both. When one experiences all the states of consciousness, then he establishes himself in his essential nature—Pure Consciousness—and realizes that he is the all-knower. Then he acquires the knowledge that the Pure Consciousness flows on various degrees and grades, termed waking, dreaming, and sleeping. These states or modes of consciousness have arisen from their source, turīya, and finally dissolve in it. Yet the nature of Pure Consciousness, which is self-existent, never changes. It is everlasting, infinite, and changeless.

When the aspirant strengthens his practice of meditation and contemplation and learns to analyze and resolve all his desires, thoughts, and feelings through the practice of yoga-nidrā, he attains a state in which he consciously learns to place his mind in deep rest. *Yoga-nidrā* cannot be translated into any other language, but for the convenience of modern students it is called "yogic sleep" or "sleepless sleep." This is a state of conscious sleep in which the student is in deep sleep and yet remains fully conscious. Only evolved minds that are fully conscious and use methods of meditation and contemplation attain this state. Yoga-nidrā is a very useful way to enjoy a voluntary sleep unlike ordinary sleep. The yogis use this technique for sleep and meditation both, thus it is called yoga-nidrā. Yoga-nidrā is an advanced practice that can help the student to come out of sloth and inertia, which are the greatest enemies of the student and which obstruct his progress every now and then. The quality of rest one receives through this method is entirely different from that which is derived through ordinary sleep. Yoga-nidrā is a revitalizing exercise that gives total rest to the mind, brain, nervous system, senses, and body. Except through meditation and yoga-nidrā, one cannot give rest to the totality of the mind. As body, brain, and conscious mind need rest, similarly there is a necessity for resting the unconscious mind. There is no drug and no scientific or physical technique so far discovered that gives rest to the unconscious part of mind, except the technique of yoga-nidrā.

Yoga-nidrā is unlike sleep because sleep gives only partial rest and because in sleep one withdraws one's consciousness and becomes unconscious. Yoga-nidrā is unlike meditation because in meditation one does not seek conscious awareness of the state of deep sleep. It is somewhat difficult for the modern mind to comprehend all the levels of one's inner being and to attain the goal of meditation. During meditation, one learns to practice a meditative pose that is steady and comfortable, but in yoga-nidrā, the corpse pose *(śavāsana)* alone is recommended. Yoga-nidrā supports and strengthens the meditational technique. Deep meditation helps the mind attain one-pointedness, while contemplation leads one to the state of constant awareness.

Yoga-nidrā has immense benefits and can be used for learning the subtleties of life. The dimensions of life that are not explored during waking, dreaming, and sleeping can be explored through yoga-nidrā or by attaining the fourth state. It is interesting to note that the frontiers of waking, dreaming, and sleeping are not explored or understood. No one practices enough to explore those frontiers because researchers seem to be interested in exploring the world of objects and gross thought patterns and symbols only. But it is also important to explore the process by which the waking mind slips to the dreaming state and then goes to deep sleep. It is difficult to study how the conscious mind withdraws itself and goes to the lap of the unconscious state; only by practicing yoga-nidrā can one do this.

In this practice, the student learns to witness his body by withdrawing his conscious mind voluntarily. The student first learns to train his will power by building his determination *(saṅkalpa śakti)*, and then determines to voluntarily go to a state of deep sleep and come back to the fully conscious state according to his will. Careful vigilance and observation lead the student to study the incoming thoughts from the unconscious mind. The yogis recall all their samskā ras, watch them, examine, and even select and reject them according to their need. Those thought patterns that are disturbing are rejected by the yogis, and those that are helpful are strengthened. Many students of the occult and psychic phenomena may accidentally touch this state of mind, but they do not know the definite way of experiencing the same state again, and they cannot recall this experience repeatedly. A deep study of these three states—waking, dreaming, and sleeping—reveals that, with the help and practice of yoga-nidrā, one can go beyond all the levels of the unconscious.

Practicum

Yoga-nidrā is a simple method consisting of a few breathing and mental exercises. To practice it, lie down on your back in a quiet and undisturbed place in the corpse pose (śavāsana), using a pillow and covering yourself with a blanket. The surface should be hard, and the pillow should be soft. Start doing diaphragmatic breathing. After twenty inhalations and exhalations, feel as though you are inhaling by visualizing an incoming wave of the ocean and exhaling by emptying yourself with the wave going back to the ocean. After ten or fifteen breaths, the *Śavayātrā* or 61 Points Exercise should be carefully done.*

Then learn to divest yourself of thoughts, feelings, and desires, but see that you do not touch the brink of sleep. The space between the two breasts, which is called *anāhata cakra,* is the center where the mind rests during this practice. The mind should be focused on inhalation and exhalation only. While exhaling, the mind and breath are coordinated in a perfect manner. The mind observes that the inhalation and exhalation are functioning harmoniously. When the breath does not go through the stress of jerks and shallowness, and there is no unconscious expansion of the pause between inhalation and exhalation, then it establishes harmony. Beginners, for lack of practice, are trapped by inertia, and in most cases they experience going to the brink of sleep. This should be avoided in all cases. One should not pursue the practice at this state, but should just wake up and then repeat the same process the next day. This practice of emptying yourself and focusing on the breath should not be continued more than ten minutes in the beginning, and it should not be practiced more than once a day, for the mind has a habit of repeating its experience, both unconsciously and consciously. In habit formation, regularity, punctuality, and a systematic way of practice should be followed literally.

7

नान्त:प्रज्ञं न बहिष्प्रज्ञं नोभयत:प्रज्ञं न प्रज्ञानघनं न प्रज्ञं नाप्रज्ञम् ।
अदृष्टमव्यवहार्यमग्राह्यमलक्षणमचिन्त्यमव्यपदेश्य-मेकात्मप्रत्ययसारं
प्रपंचोपशमं शान्तं शिवमद्वैतं चतुर्थं मन्यन्ते स आत्मा स
विज्ञेय:।।७।।

Nāntah-prajñam na bahih-prajñam nobhayatah-prajñam
na prajñana-ghanam na prajñam nāprajñam. Adṛṣṭam-
avyavahāryam-agrāhyam-alakṣaṇam-acintyam-avyapadeśyam-
ekātma-pratyaya-sāram prapañcopa śamam śāntam śivam-
advaitam caturtham manyante sa ātmā sa vijñeyaḥ.

Turīya is the fourth state. In this state, consciousness is not
turned inward nor outward nor both. It is undifferentiated;
it is beyond the spheres of cognition and non-cognition.
This state cannot be experienced through the senses or
known by comparison or inference; it is incomprehensible,
unthinkable, and indescribable. This is Pure Consciousness.
This is the real Self. It is the cessation of all phenomena; it is
tranquil, all-blissful, and one without second. This real Self
is to be realized.

Turīya is that state in which consciousness is aware of
and yet remains aloof from the other three states of waking,
dreaming, and sleeping. In this state, the mind is neither
inwardly nor outwardly directed. Consciousness maintains
its all-encompassing awareness and spontaneously realizes
a total reintegration of all levels of reality. This state is
attributeless, eternal, and unchanging and is beyond the
conditions of cause and effect. It cannot be comprehended
by the mind; it cannot be compared with anything; it cannot
be perceived, inferred, thought, or described. Yet it is not a
void but is the state beyond the void. It is the very nature of
consciousness, the center of supreme peace, bliss, and
Absolute Reality. This is the Self, and it has to be realized
because this is the purpose of life.

There is a very fine line of demarcation between deep
sleep and samādhi. In samādhi, which is a deep state of
meditation, the aspirant remains fully conscious though
tranquil, and in deep sleep the student remains tranquil but
unconscious. In both states, deep sleep and samādhi, the
aspirant remains very close to the Reality, but in sleep he is
unconscious, while in samādhi he is fully conscious. In deep
sleep, he is not aware of his existence, while in samādhi,
constant awareness remains uninterrupted. One experiences a different reality in each case. In the state of turīya,
the aspirant goes beyond the sphere of sleep and samādhi
both. He experiences oneness with the Supreme Consciousness and witnesses the transitory world as quite
different from his essential nature.

In this state of wisdom, one knows all the states, yet
turīya is beyond all of them. As the mind is beyond the
senses, the center of consciousness, turīya, is beyond all the
states of mind. This state is neither internal not external nor

can any simile describe it. In this state, there is nothing like becoming; there is only purely being. The realized one alone enjoys this perennial state of eternal bliss. Neither sense perceptions, thoughts, feelings, nor desires are able to explain this state of realization. Turīya is a state in which the knower knows and knows that he knows. Suppose a thirsty person is in search of water. He goes to the place where he can quench his thirst; but when water is everywhere, one has not to search for a fountain of water.

8

सोयमात्माध्यक्षरमोंकारोधिमात्रं पादा मात्रा मात्राश्च पादा
अकार उकारो मकार इति ।।८।।

*So'yam-ātmā'dhyakṣaram-omkaro'dhimātram pādā
mātrā mātrāś-ca pādā akāra ukāro makāra iti.*

Pure Consciousness, which has been described as having
four states, is indivisible. It is Om. The sounds *A-U-M* (ah,
ou, mm) and the letters *A, U, M* are the three states of
waking, dreaming, and sleeping, and these three states are
the three sounds and letters. But the fourth state, which is
unknown and hidden, is realized only in silence.

That Supreme Consciousness is the Ātman, the Self. The Self is identical with the eternal syllable Om. Consciousness is experienced by the individual self on three different levels, but there is a fourth state that is beyond the comprehension of the mind. Thus, consciousness is thought to have three states and a state beyond, turīya. From this point of view, the eternal syllable, Om, also has three phonemes, *A-U-M,* representing three states, and silence, representing the fourth state, turīya.

Om consists of three sounds, *A-U-M,* denoting the gross, the subtle, and the causal aspects of Ultimate Truth. When one is able to analyze the experiences of the different states of consciousness and, at the same time, of consciousness in its totality, then one attains the fourth state, turīya. Through contemplation on *A-U-M,* the three sound symbols of the three states of the individual self—the student is endowed with the qualifications required for understanding the fourth state, turīya.

The explanation of Om depends on the linguistic significance of its three constituents *A, U,* and *M. A* and *U* are simple vowels. In the Sanskrit alphabet, *A* is the first vowel and serves as the gateway for the manifestation of all other vowels and consonants. It is identical with the soft aspirate sound, which is the sound of the breath and the grossest manifestation of the life force, or prāna. In Indian

---

See page 110 for the description of Śavayātrā, the 61 Points Exercise, and for the application of this exercise as a method of intuitive diagnosis for individuals for personal use and for professional application by psychologists, physicians, and counselors.

mythology, the phoneme *A* represents the progenitor or creator, while *U* is identical with the preserver, and *M* represents the annihilator. The sound *A* is the ever in-and out-flowing, all-embracing vital force, and the vowel *U* is the deep vibrating force which is the lower limit in the tonal scale of the human voice. It is the threshold of silence that merges into *M,* the final sound. *M* in Sanskrit is called *anusvāra,* which is a phoneme that stands between consonants and vowels and is represented by a dot, a point above the consonant or vowel. Thus, it is a symbol of the unity, totality, imperishability, and indestructibility of the Absolute. It is the sonorous, inwardly directed, final vibrating sound of Om. After these phonemes, *A-U-M,* there remains a state of silence that, by its very nature, cannot be expressed by any means. Thus the sound Om is representative of all the levels of consciousness involved in manifestation, preservation, annihilation, and the fourth state, turīya.

During the Upanishadic period, many ceased the quest to understand the higher philosophical meaning of Om through proper study and direct spiritual realization. This eternal sound is currently very popular, but the tradition of practicing it properly has almost faded out. It is now spoken, sung, written, and otherwise utilized indiscriminately, but only contemplation and meditation on the syllable Om leads one to realize the *summum bonum* of life. Simply repeating the sound Om technically like a parrot is not very beneficial, just as repeating *God* all day without understanding its importance or having a feeling for it is meaningless. Those who practice this syllable and contemplate and meditate upon it know that this is the only sound that can be produced after sealing the teeth and lips, no matter which word from any language is intended to be hummed. Hum any sound or any syllable or word—it comes out as the sound Om.

When an aspirant practices the sound Om to attain a one-pointed mind, he does not find any difficulty in coordinating this sound with the breath. Any other sound coordinated with the breath creates jerks in the breath and obstructs its serene flow, and when the breath flow is disturbed, its counterpart—the mind or thinking process— is also disturbed. When aspirants concentrate on the breath flow and coordinate the syllable Om, they prepare themselves for the voyage that leads them to the finer states within. The aspirant knows that *A* represents waking, *U* dreaming, and *M* sleeping, but he wants to attain the fourth state, turīya, by attaining the state of soundless sound that the mystics often describe as the voice of silence.

9

जागरितस्थानो वैश्वानरोकारः प्रथमा मात्राप्तेरादि-मत्त्वाद्वाप्नोति ह वै
सर्वान् कामानादिश्च भवति य एवं वेद।।९।।

Jagarita-sthāno vaiśvānaro 'kārah prathamā mātrā '-āpter-ā
dimattvād-vāpnoti ha vai sarvān kāmān-ādiś-ca bhavati ya
evam veda.

The consciousness experienced during the waking state is *A,*
the first letter of Om. It pervades all other sounds. Without
the first syllable *A,* one cannot utter the word Om, and
likewise, without knowing the waking state, one cannot
know the other states of consciousness. One who is aware of
this reality fulfills all his desires and is successful.

The first phoneme, *A,* is of the same nature as the waking state (vaiśvānara). It is the all-pervading simple vowel; all sounds are pervaded by *A.* The first letter of Om is also compared with the manifest universe because one is aware of the phenomenal world through the conscious waking state. When the knowledge of the phenomenal world is revealed through contemplation and meditation, one becomes capable of attaining one's desired objects and becomes *āpta-kāma*—one whose desires are all fulfilled. Through deep contemplation and meditation, a student becomes aware of the unity of the life force, prana, permeating the diversity of the universe. The aspirant, instead of perceiving different names and forms, experiences the life force alone, which is one of the aspects of the manifestation of consciousness.

To be successful in the world of objects, one should learn to cultivate the full use of one's conscious mind. Though the conscious part of the mind is a small part of mind, it functions during the waking state. During this time, the mind employs the senses to contact the phenomenal world; all sense impressions are received during this state. The knowledge of the external world is also important, and if this knowledge is acquired, then it inspires one to seek another level of knowledge. The external world is the world of means, and one who knows how to utilize the conscious mind and apply it to acquire some worldly object is successful. The idea here is how to make the best use of the conscious mind so that external amenities are successfully acquired and the necessities of daily life are met. The world of phenomena should also be understood and dealt with. Though one may know that the waking state does not give comprehensive knowledge of the other dimensions of life, it is important to understand, utilize, and direct the conscious part of mind that functions during the waking state. Without this, one cannot successfully maintain relationships or have the means for attaining worldly goals. There are two views of how to utilize the objects of the world. One view is to make all the objects of the world means for attaining the highest state of consciousness, and the other view is to understand the phenomenal world and make use of it in a way that it does not create a barrier for the aspirant. In the first case, the time, energy, and skill that are utilized in having the necessary means for maintaining a healthy body and environment seem to be important. But more important from the standpoint of sādhāna is to know how to live skillfully so that the charms, temptations, and attractions of the world do not create obstacles in the path of enlightenment. After gaining knowledge of the phenomenal world, the aspirant knows that everything in the external world is subject to change. On some level, the objects of the world have value and are apparently real, but, in actuality, they do not exist as they are. Their form changes, and, therefore, their names change and their qualities also change. When an aspirant adjusts himself to this realization, he practices his sādhāna by understanding the apparent reality and does not become attached to the phenomenal world or waste his time and energy in acquiring more worldly objects than the bare necessities. To have only the bare necessities of life can become a means on the path of enlightenment.

The second view for utilizing the objects of the world is to use them as means so they do not create barriers on the path of unfoldment. Less importance is given to the external world, and no attachment is allowed to be strengthened toward the objects of the world. In both cases, attachment is considered to be the main barrier. When the aspirant adjusts himself to the external environment of the transitory world, then he knows the way of utilizing and approaching all the means of the world as a part of sādhāna for attaining his goal, which is turīya. He can use all the means without establishing ownership over the objects of the world. Without cultivating this attitude, it becomes impossible for him to be nonattached and thus to have control over the sense gratifications. The external world is the world of pleasures and pains—the pair of opposites. From where arises pleasure also arises pain. The aspirant desires to attain a state of freedom from the pairs of opposites and so examines the phenomenal world, but he does not find himself fulfilled. Therefore, he intensifies his search toward other dimensions of consciousness.

The conscious state of mind, if skillfully utilized during the waking state, fulfills one's desires in the external world. Those who know how to direct their energy to be successful in the external world know how to direct the conscious mind and make the best use of the waking state. After collecting data from various quarters, it is evident that ordinary people are not as satisfied and happy as they appear. Though they have more than they need, yet they are afraid of the unknown, and they do not know how to go beyond the mire of delusion created by the pairs of opposites. The highest of joys that human beings can acquire during the waking state is sexual union, in which the partners receive a glimpse of joy, but that joy is only brief and partial. For want of the expansion of this joy, human beings work hard and gather together all sorts of means, but none of these helps them to attain the state of freedom, perennial happiness. Those who are awakened search for this perennial happiness and explore other states of consciousness. One who knows how to make use of the waking state skillfully can have success in the phenomenal world, but this success does not enlighten anyone. There are people who are not aware enough to feel the necessity to explore other dimensions of consciousness. They want to have shortcuts for attaining happiness, but they do not have inner ability, and so they do not comprehend the higher levels of consciousness. Such people look for many ways to escape and are not successful in the world. Either they become fanatic or they join a cult, which is unhealthy and is considered to be religious sickness. The best of people are those fortunate few who literally renounce the world and devote their time and energy to explore the higher dimensions of consciousness. Such people are rare and are worthy of reverence.

It has already been explained that the path of renunciation and the path of action are both fruitful and useful for enlightenment. Nonattachment and constant awareness are two requisites in both paths. It is a fact that the path of action is more time-consuming than the path of renunciation. In the path of action, one directs his energy to acquire means, and in the path of renunciation, one has ample time to devote one's energy to the attainment of his goal. Those who are on the path of action suffer if they do not perform their duties skillfully and selflessly. Thus they become victims of their own deeds and actions. Likewise, those renunciates who have not renounced the lustful attitude toward the objects of the world also suffer. Therefore, it is not the path, but it is the attitude that one builds for treading one of the paths with full sincerity, devotion, and perseverance. There are some renunciates who renounce the objects of the cares and pleasures of the world with full sincerity, but then they do not persistently practice their sādhāna. Their minds deepen the grooves of inert habits, and thus they become the victims of sloth and inertia.

Off and on in human life, there comes an occasion when one receives a glimpse of the transitory and apparent reality of this universe. If such opportunities are utilized by practicing nonattachment during those moments, one will surely attain his goal. This awakening comes in every human mind. There is nothing in the world—no relationship, no object—that can fulfill the human desire to have everlasting peace, bliss, and happiness. The moments of awakening make everyone aware of the truth, but for lack of practice, constant awareness towards truth remains absent. Thus, human beings suffer on account of their self-created miseries.

In this verse, the waking state is explained as being compared with the world of phenomena, which is related to the first letter of Om, *A*. But to know the comprehensive meaning of Om, one should learn other aspects of consciousness related to *U* and *M*, and finally to the hidden state of Om, the supreme state of silence.

स्वप्नस्थानस्तैजस उकारो द्वितीया मात्रोत्कर्षादुभयत्वाद्वो-त्कर्षति ह वै
ज्ञानसन्ततिं समानश्च भवति नास्याब्रह्मवित् कुले भवति य एवं
वेद।।१०।।

Svapna-sthānas-taijasa ukāro dvitīyā mātrotkarṣād-ubhayatvād-votkarṣāti ha vai jñāna-santatim samānaś-ca bhavati nāsyābrahma-vit kule bhavati ya evam veda.

The consciousness experienced during the dreaming state is *U*, the second letter of Om. This is an elevated intermediate state between the waking and sleeping states. One who knows this subtler state is superior to others. One who knows this—in his family knowers of Brahman will be born.

The second phoneme, *U,* is of the same nature as the dreaming reality (taijasa). When the aspirant becomes capable of analyzing and realizing the nature of *U* and the dreaming reality through deep contemplation and meditation, he attains knowledge of and mastery over his unconscious mind.

After analyzing the nature of the mind and its modifications, the aspirant becomes aware of the subtle impressions, or samskāras, that create all the objects of dreams. The aspirant then overcomes negative mental attitudes such as animosity, jealousy, and hatred. Being the middle phoneme, *U,* the intermediate state, is more subtle than and superior to *A,* the first. It deals with the world as being comprised of ideas rather than objects and is thus closer to the Truth. This world of ours is an idea. Without an idea, creativity is lost in bewilderment. It is the idea that builds the worldly structure for human beings. Therefore, idea is the architect and is superior to the construction. Such an aspirant who realizes the state of *U* can inspire others, for he unfolds the mystery of ideas and creativity both.

The waking reality is always considered to be a creative and dynamic state, for one has the opportunity and instrumentation to express oneself in the external world. The entire educational system is devoted to the cultivation of this state, for life is divided into two aspects—within and without. It is important to manage the external aspect of life for three reasons: a) it might become the means for gaining higher knowledge and satisfying the sense gratifications; b) it gives knowledge of the phenomenal world and its transitory nature, which inspires the mind of the aspirant to search through other dimensions of life; and the waking state is a conscious state, and if the aspirant learns to use this state for contemplation and meditation, it gives him the power of expanding his field of experience compared to those who do not meditate and contemplate.

The experiencer experiences waking, dreaming, and sleeping realities, and during these experiences, finds himself absorbed in that particular state and unaware of the other states. When he analyzes his role in different states as sleeper, dreamer, and cognizer of the external world, he wonders and wants to comprehend the entire field of consciousness and witnesses it collectively by attaining a state beyond. After examining the waking state, he likes to examine consciousness during the dreaming state. During dreams, one is not aware of the phenomenal world the way he is aware during the waking state because his body and senses are at rest, and his conscious mind is also moving toward the sleeping state. In this state, only the past memories from the unconscious are recalled. Actually, no one can determine dreaming. If someone determines to dream about something, it is not possible for him to dream the way he wants. The determination that is built during the waking state is not applied to the reality of the dreaming state. One can give suggestions to oneself and then can recall those suggestions and think that he can train himself and dream the way he wants. But actually the dreaming state is beyond the control of the ordinary person's conscious mind. When the experiencer is not in touch with the objects of the world, his senses do not perceive fresh impressions from them. During that state of mind, the flow of those suppressions and repressions comes forward. Though it is an interruption while one's mind is moving toward the sleeping state, yet it offers an opportunity for one to analyze his desires, motivations, feelings, and thoughts.

At this stage, the mind ponders over unfulfilled desires, feelings, and attachments. The dream world is unique in itself, and in it the prominent habits of mind can be analyzed. Deep-rooted desires cause frequent and repetitive dreams. If there is no desire or want to fulfill, there will be no necessity to dream. Dream is the product of those desires that are unfulfilled. The mind travels to the grooves of its unfulfilled desires and creates a predominant habit pattern. Thus dreams can be worth analyzing to help one understand the predominant habits of one's mind. But again, there are varieties of habits, and sometimes the aspirant thinks that he has complete control over his thoughts, desires, and feelings. But again he finds that there are dark corners of the unconscious mind where still lie some hidden desires. Suppose one has apparently vacuumed the carpet of his living room, and it looks very neat and clean; but if he lifts up the corner of the carpet, he will find that a layer of dirt is hidden beneath. So is the case with the unconscious mind. When an aspirant goes through various levels of unconsciousness, a time comes when his whole mind becomes topsy-turvy. But a burning desire for attaining the goal of life can annihilate the other desires, feelings, and thoughts. In such a case, one goes beyond this turmoil and experiences that higher dimension for which he was longing.

The mind also has the quality of pacifying itself no matter how difficult a problem may be. That which cannot be dealt with by the mind during the waking state is dealt with during the dreaming state. That is why it is called a more subtle state than the waking state. This state is therapeutic because in it one has opportunity to express oneself the way one wants to. All the unfulfilled desires, thoughts, and feelings which for any reason are not fulfilled during the waking state, create a dreaming reality. One cannot dream of something that he has never seen, imagined, heard of, or read about. The individual self experiences many dimensions of reality, and the dreaming reality is one of them. During dreaming, the mind wants to bring forward and express those ideas, desires, thoughts, and feelings which for some reason could not be expressed during the waking state. One cannot understand the dreaming state merely by analyzing a few dreams. During the dreaming state, one completely forgets what he was in the waking state. One is rewarded in the dreaming state and is whipped in the dreaming state, so both rewards and punishments are given at a more subtle or mental level during the dreaming state. It is a finer state than the waking state.

One can magnify all of one's desires and fears in dreams because dreaming is a self-created state. Many people dream in the daytime; therefore, the waking reality is compared by the sages to the dreaming reality. For the wise, both states are alike because they give only a partial glimpse of the totality. That which one acquires in the conscious waking state vanishes in the dreaming state, and that which is acquired in the dreaming state vanishes in the waking state. Desire does not really vanish in the dreaming state, but it seems to vanish when one goes to deep sleep. Actually, desire does not vanish even in deep sleep; one is simply not aware of one's desires in this state. Desire really vanishes only when one attains the fourth state, turīya. Then it is resolved, it is understood, it is analyzed because there all one's desires are fulfilled. In waking, one obtains objects of the phenomenal world and achieves external success, but in turīya one experiences completeness. One no longer desires anything lower once he has attained something higher.

All the great laws of physics have been discovered in the contemplative state, and the unique works of art and literature are the products of the contemplative mind. Meditation and contemplation both require a one-pointed mind, but the difference is that during meditation and contemplation, one consciously places himself in a concentrated and undisturbed state. During the dreaming state, there is no control, and one is not conscious the way one is conscious and in control in the waking state. Control here measures the ability of focusing the mind toward its desired goal. There are varieties of dreams, but here it is the entire dream state and the reality that is experienced during it that are being discussed.

During meditation, one remains fully awake and conscious, but during dreaming, one is not conscious, and the unconscious impressions appear whether one desires them to do so or not. In the dreaming state, one has no control, but in meditation one has perfect control. When it is said that one can remain fully conscious while dreaming, it means that one can remain in meditation and recall all the unfulfilled desires that are expressed during that time. One can then analyze and resolve them. In comparing meditation with the dreaming state, one notes that the mind is made inward in meditation and is not allowed to slip to the valley of inertia or imagine about the future. The mind is trained to maintain the single focal point of meditation voluntarily. This gives the aspirant an opportunity to judge, analyze, and decide the usefulness of the impressions coming from the unconscious that create dreaming reality. This is an intermediate state between sleeping and waking in which the ordinary mind remains in a semiconscious state. One is neither in deep sleep nor is he awake. During meditation, the meditator can experience all that which is experienced during the dreaming state. He is fully conscious though he is not utilizing his senses and not contacting external objects. When the conscious state is expanded, dream analysis becomes clear, and the ideas and symbols that are experienced during that state are easily understood. From a sādhāna viewpoint, dreams are divided into two categories—those which are helpful to one's sādhāna and those that are harmful to one's sādhāna. Impressions or ideas from the waking state that appear during the dreaming state can be helpful and can be injurious both. If one has clear introspection, the harmful and injurious dreams that strain and distract the mind and its energy can be analyzed and resolved. All conflicts that are at the root of dreams can also be resolved. A time comes when meditation stirs the unconscious mind and brings forward impressions from its hidden recesses. It quickens the method of analyzing, understanding, and surveying the whole dreaming state. Whatever dream reality is, it can be brought under the meditator's conscious control. That aspect of mind that dreams and the energy that is consumed by dreaming can be brought into creative use and channeled for higher purposes. People dream their whole lives, but the dreaming state does not help anyone in the attainment of enlightenment. Meditators do not dream. Of course, sometimes they experience a sort of dream that can be called a prophetic dream, but during meditation the mind is focused on one object, and it flows uninterruptedly toward that object only. Thoughts, ideas, feelings, and desires do flow from the unconscious mind, but they do not have any power to disturb the meditator because his mind is concentrated. Those impressions are like other thoughts that pass through the mind, but they do not create disturbance for the meditator. But the dreamer may be disturbed by his dreams because they are not under his conscious control. Actually this śruti makes the aspirant aware that dreams alone are not the subject for analysis but that the entire dreaming reality should be understood thoroughly.

The dreaming state is represented by the letter *U*, which comes between *A* and *M*. For knowing Om in a comprehensive way, one has to move to higher dimensions of consciousness. The higher dimension here means that the meditator also desires to know the sleeping state. This state is represented by the letter *M*, the last letter of Om. After examining all the joys and pleasures of the external world, finally one delights to have a deeper quality of joy during sleep. Consciousness withdraws itself from the waking state and the dreaming state and goes to the restful state of unconsciousness.

11

सुषुप्तस्थानः प्राज्ञो मकारस्तृतीया मात्रा मितेरपीतेर्वा मिनोति ह वा इदँ
सर्वमपीतिश्च भवति य एवं वेद ।।११।।

Susupta-sthānah prājño makāras trtīyā mātrā miter-apīter
vā minoti ha vā idam sarvam-apītiś-ca bhavati ya evam
veda.

The consciousness experienced during the deep state of
sleep is *M*, the third letter of Om. One who knows this more
subtle state as well is able to comprehend all within himself.

The third phoneme *M* is the deep sleep state (prājña). By constantly remembering Om, *A* and *U* become one sound and submerge into M The pronunciation becomes *OMOMOMOM;* thus, *A* and *U* are dissolved into *M* and again are evolved from *M.* In this way, prājña, *M,* is the source that contains and measures *A* and *U,* which emerge from and merge into it. One who realizes that the phoneme *M* is identical to prājña becomes capable of realizing the nature of the internal and external worlds. He is also able to realize his oneness with the entire universe.

The sleeping state indicates that consciousness has power to withdraw and expand itself. One who knows that it functions both externally and internally is definitely superior to one who has explored only the waking and dreaming states.

A real meditator does not sleep the way ordinary creatures sleep; sleep is brought under his voluntary control and will. He determines to sleep and then to wake up whenever he wants. This is the art of yoga-nidrā, which is practiced by meditators. During ordinary sleep, the mind remains withdrawn from the dreaming and waking states. This restful period is essential for healthy living. But it is not necessary to waste eight to twelve hours for sleep and yet not have restful sleep. Such a supposed need is a mere myth and a tradition without truth. The human body, even after exhaustion and fatigue, does not need more than three hours of sleep, provided that the art of sleep is practiced rightly. Wasting time and energy leads one to the formation of the fabric of inertia and sloth, which is not helpful even for ordinary people. Actually, the quality of sleep counts more than the number of hours slept.

To attain the fourth state, one has to go through the

unconscious dimension of life. Many writers, for the sake of pleasing readers, say that the unconscious mind is bypassed, and that the fourth state is attainable without diving into the unconscious. But that is only talk—mere empty words without experiential knowledge. The difference between sleep and samādhi has already been explained. The sleeping state is more subtle than the waking and dreaming states, and one who knows how to utilize this state can benefit himself immensely. He can give rest to his body, nervous system, brain, and mind, and he can expand his consciousness and know that which is unknown to ordinary minds.

Although the mind is at rest, it is not empty; the mind never remains empty—either one is sleeping, dreaming, or awake, or else one is having a vision, or hallucinating, or fantasizing. During deep sleep, there is the experience of the void; the same void can be experienced during meditation. That void is not empty, but there is a feeling of emptiness. During that time, there is no content, and that is why it is called deep sleep. So sleep is an unconscious state without content; there is no awareness. When one is in the void, he does not know that he is in the void, but once awake, he remembers being in the void. In deep meditation, one is in the void and is aware of it at the time. The meditative state is a fully awakened state.

There are two laws that can be noticed in daily life: the law of expansion and the law of contraction. When one follows the law of contraction, one becomes a victim of petty-mindedness and suffers on account of destructive emotions. One builds boundaries around himself and only feeds his individual ego, that which no doubt helps to retain individuality, but which also keeps him separated from the whole. By following the law of expansion, one goes on expanding one's consciousness to the extent of Universal Consciousness, and then one loves all and remains in perennial joy all the time. The experiences of this dimension are very subtle. Such a fortunate one who has already explored the waking, dreaming, and sleeping realities is a highly evolved aspirant, and he prepares himself for the last part of the voyage, turīya.

A Comparative Study of Meditation and Contemplation

Om is the subtlest and finest syllable for focusing the mind and making it one-pointed and inward. It is used for meditation by those who have totally renounced their desires for worldly cares and pleasures and who are seeking nothing but enlightenment. Preceptors also impart the knowledge of many great statements of the Upanishads, called *mahāvākyas,* to students for the practice of contemplation.

The barriers created by the mind, senses, and sense objects obscure the vision of the aspirant. As long as the mind continues to interact with the senses, its dissipating nature cannot be brought under control. The mind seems to have a dual nature: either it functions with the help of the senses in the external world, or it recalls the impressions stored in the unconscious mind. Through sādhāna, the mind uses a center of focus so that it is not disturbed by its outgoing tendency or its habit of recalling the impressions already stored. So voluntary withdrawal of the senses becomes one of the primary steps of sādhāna. When desires for obtaining worldly objects are present, the aspirant can easily withdraw the mind from the objects of the world and gradually train it not to be dissipated by sense perceptions.

Then the mind is neither distracted nor distorted and is capable of practicing contemplation and meditation. The mind can then be trained to concentrate on the sound Om until it becomes an unconscious habit and a part of life for the aspirant. Constant *japa* leads to a state of *ajapā japa,* in which one remembers Om constantly. This state of mind can be cultivated by being aware of the syllable Om even while doing one's daily duties. Aspirants who practice Om in this manner are not disturbed by the travails of life, for they have created an inner refuge for the mind. If such a center for the mind is not cultivated, it is dissipated with the constant distractions of the sense perceptions and the incoming flow of thoughts, feelings, and desires that are already in the storehouse of memory, the unconscious mind. When the aspirant learns to meditate on Om, the conscious mind attains a tremendous ability to concentrate, and all the faculties of mind function in a coordinated way. From the philosophical viewpoint, mind is understood by four main modifications *(antah-karana catustaya).* These are made well-coordinated by meditation, and there is perfect harmony in their functioning. This is done to try to direct the totality of an undissipated mind to fathom those levels of consciousness that are not usually known by ordinary minds.

Meditation and contemplation are two different techniques, yet they are complementary to each other. Meditation is a definite method of training oneself on all levels — body, breath, conscious mind, and unconscious mind — while contemplation builds a definite philosophy. Without the support of a solid philosophy, the method of meditation does not lead to higher dimensions of consciousness. Contemplation makes one aware of the existence of the

Reality, but Reality can be experienced only through the higher techniques of meditation. In the Vedānta system, meditation and contemplation are both used. When an aspirant tires of meditation because of lack of endurance, then he contemplates on the mahāvākyas and studies those scriptures that are helpful in the path of Self-realization and enlightenment. Contemplation, *vichāra,* complements the Vedantic way of meditation, *dhyāna.*

In Vedānta philosophy, there is a definite method used for contemplation. Ordinarily, the mind remains busy in self-dialogue, entangled in the web of its thought patterns. Because of desires, feelings, and emotions, unmanageable conflicts are created in one's mental life. But the Vedānta way of contemplating transforms the entire personality of the aspirant, for the statements, mahāvākyas, imparted by the preceptor create a dynamic change in the values of his life. These statements are compact, condensed, and abstruse śrutis and cannot be understood without the help of a preceptor who is fully knowledgeable of the scriptures and these terse texts. Only a realized teacher can impart the profundity of such knowledge in a lucid language. The thoughts, feelings, and desires which were once important to the aspirant lose their value, for he has only one goal to attain. The glory of contemplation brings a dynamic transformation to the internal states of the aspirant. This seems to be very necessary, because that which creates a barrier or becomes an obstacle for students loses its strength due to the power of contemplation, which transforms all his internal states.

First, an aspirant attentively listens to the sayings of the Upanishads from a preceptor who is Brahman-conscious all the time. In the second step, he practices vichāra (contemplation), which means that he goes to the depths of the great sayings and determines to practice them with mind, action, and speech. One-pointed devotion, full determination, and dedication lead him to the higher step called *nididhyāsana*. Here he acquires comprehensive knowledge of the Ultimate Truth. But he has not yet attained the final step of consciousness that leads him to the direct realization of the one self-existent Truth without second. The highest state of contemplation is called *sākṣā-tkāra*. In this state, perception and conceptualization are in complete agreement, and all the doubts from all levels of understanding vanish forever. At this height of knowledge, truth reveals itself to the aspirant, and perfect realization is accomplished, "I am Ātman—I am Brahman." This state of advaita is attained by the process of contemplation.

Meditation plays an entirely different role and helps the aspirant make his mind one-pointed, inward, and steady. Steadiness and stillness are practiced from the very beginning in this meditational method. The method of sitting, the method of breathing, the method of concentration, and the method of allowing a concentrated mind to flow uninterruptedly are subsequent steps that help the aspirant to expand his capacity so that he can contemplate without distraction.

Contemplation

In the traditional Vedantic practice of the mahāvāk-yas, each statement is thoroughly contemplated and integrated into the personality. The course of contemplation is divided into four parts that are actually the four states of sādhāna based on the mahāvākyas. In the first stage, the student is made aware of the transient nature of the phenomenal world—*Brahma satyam jagan mithyā* (The universe is unreal; Brahman is real). The second step of contemplation is based on the knowledge of Brahman as the Absolute Truth behind all transient phenomena, and the student realizes unity in diversity—*Ekam-evādvitīyam brahma* (There is only one Brahman without second). In the third stage, he contemplates on the Absolute Reality within himself—*Aham brahmāsmi* (I am Brahman). In the fourth state, he realizes that there is only one Absolute Truth, which is self-existent and all-pervading, within and without both—*Sarvam khalvidam brahma* (All this is Brahman). When one carefully studies these statements and ponders over their meaning, one comes to know that these are contemplative and attainable states of sādhāna. The profundity of these statements or mahāvākyas cannot be comprehended by mere debate or discussion, for philosophical discussions do not help one to directly experience the inner state of wisdom. This is the way that the aspirant contemplates in order to establish a definite philosophy and realize his essential nature, which is peace, happiness, and bliss.

Inner Dialogue

Inner dialogue, a contemplative method, sometimes replaces meditation. Such dialogues strengthen the faculty of decisiveness and sharpen the buddhi (higher intellect), which can penetrate into the subtleties of the inner levels. Mental dialogue is very healthy for resolving many conflicts that arise in the mind of the aspirant as it remains habitually traveling to the grooves of his past habits. Practice of the first step in this process is described in the following example:

> Close the eyes and ask, "O mind, witness the world of objects, and observe the impermanence of those objects you long to achieve, to embrace, and to save. What difference is there in the objects of dreams and the objects of the waking state? What reason is there for being attached to the unreal things of the world; they are like experiences of the dreaming state. They are constantly changing, and you have no right to own them, for you can only use them. O mind, listen to the sayings of the great sages and teachers; follow in the footprints of those who have already trod the path of light and enlightenment. You will find that Truth is that which is unchangeable; Absolute Reality is that which is beyond the conditioning of time, space, and causation."

The primary step of inner dialogue is a part of contemplation. It inspires the aspirant in his search for knowledge. Vedānta says that knowledge that does not reveal the object as it is, is not knowledge at all, and acquiring mere information is unfulfilling. Nonattachment and practice are the most effective tools in the quest for real knowledge. Contemplation is not a method of escaping from the realities of life; rather through the process of contemplation, one makes a strong mental resolution on which he builds his whole philosophy of life.

The Vedantic way of contemplation should not be used by those who are unprepared, for they will not gain anything but confusion. Those who have decided to have freedom from ignorance and to tread the path of enlightenment should alone make these attempts. All the preliminaries that prepare the student should be practiced before one contemplates on the mahāvākyas.

Meditation

Every method of spiritual sādhāna has a definite discipline without which nothing is accomplished. The Vedānta way of meditation is different than any other method of meditation. Though all the methods of meditation are applied to understand, know, and fathom all the states of consciousness, the Vedantic method of meditation is advaita-oriented — no subtle or gross, no concrete or abstract object, except Om, is to be chosen for attaining a meditative state. The mind already remains preoccupied with innumerable thought patterns, symbols, fancies, and fantasies. To create one more is a sheer waste of time and energy and does not serve any purpose. The mind has a habit of resting upon some object, and the sound and syllable Om is the finest of all for strengthening concentration, meditation, and one's philosophy of life.

The preliminaries that are followed by other schools of meditation are also followed by the Vedānta method. These include sitting in a steady and comfortable posture with the head, neck, and trunk straight, and learning to breathe diaphragmatically, so that the motion of the lungs is regulated and the involuntary system is brought under conscious control. Ordinarily the involuntary system is not under conscious control because the irregularity of the motion of the lungs due to uneven breathing disturbs the pumping station (the heart) that supplies blood to the brain. The brain is the seat of the mind, and if the heart is disturbed, the mind is also disturbed. When the lake of mind is disturbed, one cannot clearly see what is at the bottom of the lake. When the conscious mind is disturbed, the potentials of the unconscious mind cannot be evaluated, and creativity cannot be brought forward and expressed in daily life. Therefore, disciplining the body and practicing stillness, as well as regulating the motion of the lungs with the help of harmonious breath, are both important. Regulating the body, breath, and conscious mind does not give spiritual wisdom to the aspirant. But if these are not disciplined, they disturb the aspirant, and he cannot be free to fathom the higher levels of consciousness. Though preliminary, this discipline is very important.

To have a steady posture, the aspirant chooses a particular pose that is both comfortable and straight. *Siddhasana, sukhasana,* and *svastikāsana* are recommended most frequently by the teachers of meditation. For dedicated aspirants, siddhāsana—the accomplished pose—alone is recommended. *Padmāsana,* or the lotus posture, is symbolic and is a good exercise, but often it has been seen to create disturbances in the pranic vehicles if the *bandhas* (locks) are not properly applied. Of course, a comfortable seat, and a clean, airy, and quiet place, should be carefully chosen for meditation.

Inner happiness and calmness are attained and no perspiration, twitching, or shaking are felt or observed in this method. For establishing harmonious breathing, the inhalation and exhalation of Om help the aspirant immensely. After establishing a pattern of serene, calm breathing in a steady, comfortable posture, the meditator learns to deal with the conscious part of the mind. The conscious part of the mind is that aspect that human beings use during the waking state. All the sense perceptions received during the waking state are stored in the unconscious part of the mind, which is a vast reservoir of memory. Only a fortunate few know how not to be affected by sense perceptions, feelings, and desires that are recalled in the dreaming state. During the waking state, one does not fulfill all his desires, so unfulfilled desires remain in the bed of memory, and whenever the conscious mind rests and relaxes, these impressions of unfulfilled desires come up. During the dreaming state, the mind remains withdrawn from the objects of the world because the senses are not utilized by the mind. External impressions and stimuli are not perceived and conceived during this time, but still the mind goes through vivid experiences of previously stored ideas, desires, feelings, and thoughts.

The aspect of mind that is involved in the dreaming state can be brought under control through meditation. The conscious mind and its field can be expanded, and such an expansion is helpful for the aspirant in fathoming higher levels. In this method of meditation, any fantasy or superficial experience is discarded as it comes to the surface of the meditator's mind from the hidden levels of the unconscious. Therefore, an experience of any type is considered to be invalid until the mind is completely purified and mental dissipations are brought under conscious control. Calmness of mind, peace, and happiness are the only signs of progress that encourage the meditator. Seeing visions and symbols or receiving hunches—even if they are true—are totally discarded, and these obstacles are considered to be distractions. No *siddhi* or miracle is accepted as a part of Vedantic sādhāna. The vision of the ordinary mind is different from the vision of the meditator. The vision of the meditator has clarity, but the vision of the dreamer or the ordinary mind remains clouded. When meditation deepens, the unconscious part of mind and the sleeping state are also gradually brought under control. Sleep is a necessity for the human body, senses, breath, and mind. If the unconscious mind is not at rest, and if there is constant turmoil, then the mind is unbalanced. When the conscious mind is agitated by the incoming flow of unfulfilled desires, thoughts, and feelings, the senses are not able to perceive as they should. If the conscious mind is free from conflicts, then it coordinates with the senses, and the data that are collected through sense perception are accurate. Conflicts are created in the conscious mind through a lack of decisiveness, and the mind loses its capacity to coordinate the senses. If sense perception is incorrect, conceptualization will be faulty, so it is necessary to resolve mental conflicts in order to reestablish coordination. Those who lose mental equilibrium or who are habitually unbalanced become victims of either psychosomatic disorders or pathological behavior. If one knows how to deal with disturbing thoughts, desires, and feelings, however, then the conscious mind can direct the senses, and behavior becomes normal.

Modern psychologists use counseling techniques for dealing with such problems. But without developing one's own ability to deal with them, one will always remain dependent on counselors. One develops direct experience and the ability to deal with the mind by practicing meditation. Thus, one gradually gains confidence and knows how to deal with thoughts, desires, and feelings that create uneasiness and unrest in the unconscious mind. Meditative techniques can also be applied by counselors to help them diagnose and to help patients become more aware and independent.

Practicum

There are nine mental exercises explained in the second volume of this work. It is necessary to explain only one exercise here—Śavayātrā, which helps the mind become inward and orderly. In this exercise, the mind is directed and focused on specific points of the body that help the student to survey his weak areas. The mind closely inspects the body and can discover where problems lie. This method of diagnosis has never been found to be incorrect. The medical student or the student of psychotherapy can find this exercise very useful. The method of intuitive diagnosis can be independently developed on the basis of these exercises, but sincere effort with constant practice should be made, and experiments should be conducted before these techniques are used in diagnosis. Those students who are not aware of inner potentials, abilities, and capacities might dismiss this idea as a hoax, but psychology today is not fully developed due to the lack of experimentation and experiential knowledge. Therefore, it cannot explain such experiential phenomena. The seers of meditative and contemplative science do not use these exercises for diagnosis, but psychologists can explore the validity of the experiences for the sake of experimentation and can apply them to their counseling services.

With the help of the meditative technique, one can dive deep into the unconscious and find the principle cause of psychological disorders, without which only superficial thought patterns are analyzed and disorders cannot therefore be rooted out. When the mind is led systematically from one point to another while practicing this exercise, it assumes a position of observer, and the body becomes the object of observation. The mind has the ability and capacity to discover all the disorders of the body, and the mind can easily observe any particular point that is weak. If the mind is isolated from distractions and surveys the body in a relaxed condition, and if it is not allowed to slip to the brink of sleep, it can diagnose physical disorders as well as psychological problems. When the mind is led to a particular part of the body that is weak or in which one has an ache or a pain, it immediately forgets the traveling schedule. So a one-pointed and inward mind strengthens the ability of the student in the diagnosis of emotional problems.

Though meditative and contemplative exercises are not recommended to unbalanced students, therapists and psychologists can develop this aspect of analysis and intuitive diagnosis accurately, even without counseling patients and asking them many questions that sometimes bore and confuse them. A patient is a patient and many times does not know how to express himself or herself. In such a case, the method of intuitive diagnosis can be useful.

When Freud, Jung, and Adler used hypnosis and autosuggestion to explore the disorders of the patients, they eventually had to abandon this method. They found out that many times during the hypnotic state the patient came in touch with unknown dimensions of his or her life, and the therapist lost touch with the patient. This was such a frightening experience that they did not know how to deal with the patient anymore, so they had to abandon this method. There is a vast difference between hypnosis and

meditation. Hypnosis works totally on the basis of sugges-
tion, while in meditation and contemplation one discards
suggestions and experiences the reality as it is on various
levels. One cannot deny that hypnosis does help, but it helps
only to a certain extent. There could be a finer way of
therapy if the inner dimensions of life were explored by
therapists and psychologists.

The nine mental exercises of meditation are helpful in
going to that state of consciousness which helps one to use
intuitive diagnosis correctly. In this volume, only one
practical exercise is given to strengthen meditation and
make the mind one-pointed and inward, for the habit of the
mind is outgoing, and so it is easily dissipated by the senses.
Intuitive diagnosis means that the clinician diagnoses without using any other method of diagnosis than his intuitive
knowledge. But this process of diagnosis is as valid as
diagnosis based on collecting symptoms, gathering data,
and utilizing other clinical findings. By practicing this
exercise, a physician or psychologist can know the patient's
problems and also the way of getting rid of them.

When one is relaxed and finds quiet time in stillness,
the conscious mind is rested and relaxed. The conscious
mind, being a part of the unconscious, or being one with the
unconscious, then starts receiving impressions from the
unconscious mind, which is all-knowing and which stores,
remembers, reminds, and is the bed of memory for all
physical and mental activities. The mind is conditioned by
time, space, and causation; it is not trained to be here and
now. People do not actually realize what here and now
means—either the mind goes to the old grooves of habit or
it imagines the future. This method of meditation does not
allow the mind to recall past memories and experiences or

to imagine the future but is directed in an orderly way so that it maintains nowness. During that time, the best knowledge that one already has in the inner library of the unconscious comes forward. This knowledge is finer and more subtle and can be depended upon more than the knowledge gained through the cultivation of the conscious mind, which functions during the waking state. External methods used for diagnosis alone are not the only way of diagnosing disorders and problems, but intuitive methods are also valid, provided they are used honestly.

The student of Vedānta has a profound and fearless philosophy to support him and prevent him from becoming unbalanced. With the help of the meditation technique, he experiences the finer dimensions of energy and thus gains self-confidence and inner strength. Any kind of dependency is discarded. Just as a boat is needed to cross the river, so a competent teacher is needed at a preliminary stage. When the river is crossed, the boat remains at the bank. Then the student goes ahead and does not use his teacher as a crutch.

Students are constantly reminded and instructed by their preceptors that there is only one goal of life, and that is Ultimate Truth, which is known by attaining the fourth state. The fourth state is a fully conscious state, but that consciousness does not depend on sense perception and is not polluted by a flood of dreams. It is not at all an unconscious state but is a state of full awareness that gives the human being an ability to see things as they are within and without. By attaining this state, one does not intellectualize about the nature of the objects of the world and the Ultimate Truth hidden behind them but realizes the transitory world and the hidden unity in the diversity of objects. Expansion of the conscious mind is experienced, and the reality experienced in the dreaming state and the waking state becomes clearer.

The observer and the observed create a dualistic reality, while the aspirant's aim is to realize the Absolute Truth. Here meditation ends, and the higher step of contemplation helps one to realize that one's real self is the Self of all. One also realizes that the realities experienced during waking, dreaming, and sleeping are only apparent realities, and the self-existent reality of turīya alone is the one all-pervading reality.

The words *dhyāna* (meditation) and *nididhyāsana* (contemplation) are both used in Upanishadic literature, and there is a fine distinction between the two methods. Meditation is still a dualistic concept, but the highest state of contemplation is monistic. It leads to Self-realization, while the concept of meditation leads to samādhi, and samādhi and Self-realization are two different states. A dualistic philosophy leads the aspirant to samādhi, while Vedānta philosophy and contemplation lead one to "Thou art That."

12

अमात्रश्चतुर्थोऽव्यवहार्यः प्रपंचोपशमः शिवोद्वैत एवमोंकार आत्मैव संविशत्यात्मनात्मानं य एवं वेद ।।१२।।

Amātraś-caturtho'vyavahāryah prapancopaśamah śivo' dvaita evam-omkara ātmaiva saṃviśaty-ātmanātmanam ya evam veda.

That aspect of consciousness that is not known is the soundless aspect of Om, which is not comprehended by the ordinary mind and senses. It is the state of cessation of all phenomena, even of bliss. This is a nondual state—one without second (advaita). This is termed as the fourth state and also as the real Self. One who knows this expands himself to Universal Consciousness.

The soundless sound Om—silence—is of the same nature as the fourth state, turīya. Turīya has no parts and is incomprehensible, being beyond speech and mind. It is the state of realization in which all doubts and conflicts are resolved. It is the final state of Om into which *A-U-M* have merged. It is the nondual and blissful state that is the cessation of the influence of the grand illusion (māyā). It is identical with Ātman, the very Self of all individuals. He who knows this state of Absolute Reality expands into the Supreme Self, realizes himself as turīya, and is not born again.

All the states of consciousness explained so far—waking, dreaming, and sleeping—are the experiences of dualism, for the experiencer is different from the experience. But the fourth state, turīya, is the nondualistic state which is compared with the silent sound of Om. All sounds actually arise from silence, so this state can be termed as soundless sound. That is why it has been given the name turīya. If one stands on the bank of a river, he hears the sound of the river as it flows. When he goes back to the source of the river, he discovers that the mouth of the river creates no sound. The sound expands more and more as the river moves and expands and meets the ocean. But here the meditator is going to the origin of the sounds, which is the perfect silence—the state beyond termed as turīya. In deep meditation and contemplation, a state is attained in which truth is realized—self and real Self is realized. Such a state is inexplicable, for the weight of this truth is so heavy that the mind and speech cannot hold it. Therefore, no words can explain this perennial joy. From this height of realization, one can comprehend the knowledge of all states of consciousness collectively, and such an aspirant attains the state of enlightenment.

Glossary

Adhyātma-vāda The philosophy of realizing Real Self.

Antah-karana Inner faculties of cognition comprised of mind, ego, intellect, and the storehouse of memories and knowledge.

Anusvāra Nasal sound.

Ajapā Japa Constant awareness of one's mantra with every breath.

Aparā-brahman Individual self.

Aparā Vidyā Knowledge of apparent reality.

Āpta kāma One who's desires are all fulfilled.

Ātman Center of Supreme Consciousness.

Brahman The Absolute Reality.

Brahma-sūtra A scripture of aphorisms written by Vyāsa.

Brahma-vihāra Frolicking in Brahman, Universal Consciousness.

Buddhi Higher intellect.

Dhyāna Meditation.

Gauḍapāda A renowned scholar, yogi, and grand teacher of Shankarācārya.

Gītā A great scripture which synthesizes all systems of philosophy and practice.

Kārikā Commentary of Māṇḍūkya-Upanishad by Gaudapāda.

Mahāvākya The great statements of the Upanishads.

Māṇḍūkya Upanishad One of the Upanishads of which this book is an explanation.

Nididhyāsana Vedānta way of contemplation.

Om A syllable, sound that represents all states of consciousness.

*Padmāsana The lotus posture.

Para-brahman Universal Self, the Absolute Reality.

Parā-Vidyā Knowledge of Absolute Reality.

Prājña The state of mind in which an individual self experiences the bliss of deep sleep.

Prāṇa The vital force of life. The breath is life, and life is breath.

Sākṣātkara Self-realization.

Sankalpa-śakti Power of determination or strong will power.

Śavāsana The corpse posture—a posture for relaxation.

Shankara A great scholar, the founder of Advaita system (One Absolute without Second).

Śavayātrā A yogic technique for surveying one's own body.

Siddhāsana The accomplished posture.

Śruti Mantras or verses of Vedas and Upanishads.Literally, śruti means that (knowledge) which is heard by the inner ear of the sages in their deep meditation and contemplation.

Sukhāsana The easy posture.

Svastikāsana A comfortable meditative pose.

Taijasa The state of mind in which the individual self experiences dreaming.

Turīya Literally, turīya means fourth. In Upanishads, the term turīya is used for Absolute Reality, the Supreme Consciousness.

Upanishad The later part of Vedas is called Upanishad. Upanishads mean those profound spiritual scriptures which are studied under the guidance of an enlightened preceptor.

*Note: Siddhāsana, Sukhāsana, Padmāsana, and Svastikāsana are meditative postures. For further details see Swami Rama, *Meditation and Its Practice* (Honesdale, Pa., Himalayan Institute Press), 1998.

Vaiśvānara The state of mind in which the individual self experiences the objects of the external world.

Veda The treasury of knowledge. Vedas are the most ancient scriptures of the world.

Vichāra (Nididhyāsana) Contemplation. In this book, nididyāsana and vichāra are used synonymously.

Yoga-nidrā Yogic sleep. It is an evolved technique of going to the deep sleep voluntarily and being fully aware of the environment at the same time.

Śavayātrā

Sixty-One Points

Technique

Lie in śavāsana (the corpse pose); relax completely for one to two minutes. Bring your attention to the point between the eyebrows and think of the number "1." Keep the attention fixed on that point for one to two seconds. In the same manner, continue concentrating on the points and corresponding numbers through point 31.

Repeat the exercise twice. Practice for seven to ten days. When this exercise can be done without allowing the mind to wander, then continue through all 61 points.

Practice the 61 Points exercise after relaxation and before *prāṇāyāma*. The exercise may be begun on either the right or left side, but be consistent. If you begin (on the torso) with the right arm, then in the lower extremities also begin with the right leg. 61 Points should not be practiced when you feel sleepy or tired.

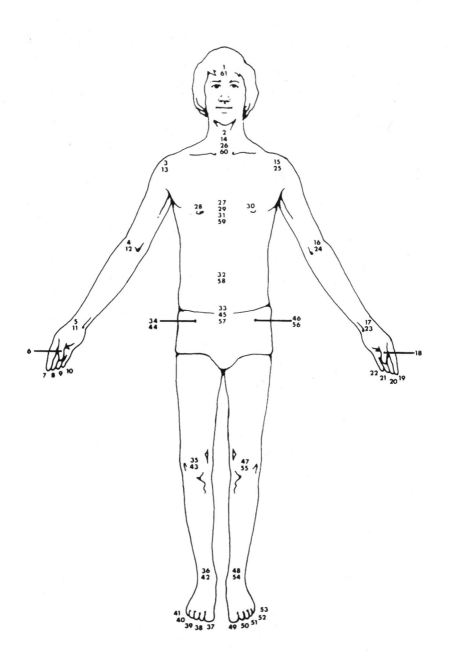

About Swami Rama

ONE OF THE greatest adepts, teachers, writers, and humanitarians of the 20th century, Swami Rama is the founder of the Himalayan Institute. Born in the Himalayas, he was raised from early childhood by the great Himalayan sage, Bengali Baba. Under the guidance of his master he traveled from monastery to monastery and studied with a variety of Himalayan saints and sages, including his grandmaster, who was living in a remote region of Tibet. In addition to this intense spiritual training, Swami Rama received higher education in both India and Europe. From 1949 to 1952, he held the prestigious position of Shankaracharya of Karvirpitham in South India. Thereafter, he returned to his master to receive further training at his cave monastery, and finally, in 1969, came to the United States, where he founded the Himalayan Institute. His best-known work, *Living with the Himalayan Masters*, reveals the many facets of this singular adept and demonstrates his embodiment of the living Himalayan Tradition.

The main building of the Himalayan Institute headquarters near Honesdale, Pennsylvania

The Himalayan Institute

A leader in the field of yoga, meditation, spirituality, and holistic health, the Himalayan Institute is a nonprofit international organization dedicated to serving humanity through educational, spiritual, and humanitarian programs. The mission of the Himalayan Institute is to inspire, educate, and empower all those who seek to experience their full potential.

Founded in 1971 by Swami Rama of the Himalayas, the Himalayan Institute and its varied activities and programs exemplify the spiritual heritage of mankind that unites East and West, spirituality and science, ancient wisdom and modern technology.

Our international headquarters is located on a beautiful 400-acre campus in the rolling hills of the Pocono Mountains of northeastern Pennsylvania. Our spiritually vibrant community and peaceful setting provide the perfect atmosphere for seminars and retreats, residential programs, and holistic health services. Students from all over the world join us to attend diverse programs on subjects such as hatha yoga, meditation, stress reduction, ayurveda, and yoga and tantra philosophy.

In addition, the Himalayan Institute draws on roots in the yoga tradition to serve our members and community through the following programs, services, and products:

Mission Programs

The essence of the Himalayan Institute's teaching mission flows from the timeless message of the Himalayan Masters, and is echoed in our on-site mission programming. Their message is to first become aware of the reality within ourselves, and then to build a bridge between our inner and outer worlds.

Our mission programs express a rich body of experiential wisdom and are offered year-round. They include seminars, retreats, and professional certifications that bring you the best of an authentic yoga tradition, addressed to a modern audience. Join us on campus for our Mission Programs to find wisdom from the heart of the yoga tradition, guidance for authentic practice, and food for your soul.

Wisdom Library and Mission Membership

The Himalayan Institute online Wisdom Library curates the essential teachings of the living Himalayan Tradition. This offering is a unique counterpart to our in-person Mission Programs, empowering students by providing online learning resources to enrich their study and practice outside the classroom.

Our Wisdom Library features multimedia blog content, livestreams, podcasts, downloadable practice resources, digital courses, and an interactive Seeker's Forum. These teachings capture our Mission Faculty's decades of study, practice, and teaching experience, featuring new content as well as the timeless teachings of Swami Rama and Pandit Rajmani Tigunait.

We invite seekers and students of the Himalayan Tradition to become a Himalayan Institute Mission Member, which grants unlimited access to the Wisdom Library. Mission Membership offers a way for you to support our shared commitment to service, while deepening your study and practice in the living Himalayan Tradition.

Spiritual Excursions

Since 1972, the Himalayan Institute has been organizing pilgrimages for spiritual seekers from around the world. Our spiritual excursions follow the traditional pilgrimage routes where adepts of the Himalayas lived and practiced. For thousands of years, pilgrimage has been an essential part of yoga sadhana, offering spiritual seekers the opportunity to experience the transformative power of living shrines of the Himalayan Tradition.

Global Humanitarian Projects
The Himalayan Institute's humanitarian mission is yoga in action—offering spiritually grounded healing and transformation to the world. Our humanitarian projects serve impoverished communities in India, Mexico, and Cameroon through rural empowerment and environmental regeneration. By putting yoga philosophy into practice, our programs are empowering communities globally with the knowledge and tools needed for a lasting social transformation at the grassroots level.

Publications
The Himalayan Institute publishes over 60 titles on yoga, philosophy, spirituality, science, ayurveda, and holistic health. These include the best-selling books *Living with the Himalayan Masters* and *The Science of Breath*, by Swami Rama; *The Power of Mantra and the Mystery of Initiation, From Death to Birth, Tantra Unveiled*, and two commentaries on the *Yoga Sutra*— *The Secret of the Yoga Sutra: Samadhi Pada* and *The Practice of the Yoga Sutra: Sadhana Pada*— by Pandit Rajmani Tigunait, PhD; and the award-winning *Yoga: Mastering the Basics* by Sandra Anderson and Rolf Sovik, PsyD. These books are for everyone: the interested reader, the spiritual novice, and the experienced practitioner.

PureRejuv Wellness Center
For over 40 years, the PureRejuv Wellness Center has fulfilled part of the Institute's mission to promote healthy and sustainable lifestyles. PureRejuv combines Eastern philosophy and Western medicine in an integrated approach to holistic health—nurturing balance and healing at home and at work. We offer the opportunity to find healing and renewal through on-site wellness retreats and individual wellness services, including therapeutic massage and bodywork, yoga therapy, ayurveda, biofeedback, natural medicine, and one-on-one consultations with our integrative medical staff.

Total Health Products
The Himalayan Institute, the developer of the original Neti Pot, manufactures a health line specializing in traditional and modern ayurvedic supplements and body care. We are dedicated to holistic and natural living by providing products using non-GMO components, petroleum-free biodegrading plastics, and eco-friendly packaging that has the least impact on the environment. Part of every purchase supports our Global Humanitarian projects, further developing and reinforcing our core mission of spirituality in action.

For further information about our programs, humanitarian projects, and products:

call: 800.822.4547
e-mail: info@HimalayanInstitute.org
write: The Himalayan Institute
          952 Bethany Turnpike
          Honesdale, PA 18431
or visit: HimalayanInstitute.org

We are grateful to our members for their passion and commitment to share our mission with the world. Become a Mission Member and inherit the wisdom of a living tradition.

HIMALAYAN INSTITUTE®

inherit the wisdom of a living tradition today!

As a Mission Member, you will gain exclusive access to our online Wisdom Library. The Wisdom Library includes monthly livestream workshops, digital practicums and eCourses, monthly podcasts with Himalayan Institute Mission Faculty, and multimedia practice resources.

Wisom Library

Netra Tantra: Harnessing Healing Force (Part 1)
Pandit Rajmani Tigunait, PhD | September 26, 2017
Read more

Mission Membership Benefits

- **Never-before-seen content from Swami Rama & Pandit Tigunait**
- **New content announcements & weekly blog roundup**
- **Unlimited access to online yoga classes and meditation classes**
- **Members only digital workshops and monthly livestreams**
- **Downloadable practice resources and Prayers of the Tradition**

Get FREE access to the Wisdom Library for 30 days!

Mission Membership is an invitation to put your spiritual values into action by supporting our shared commitment to service while deepening your study and practice in the living Himalayan Tradition.

BECOME A MISSION MEMBER AT:
himalayaninstitute.org/mission-membership/

LIVING WITH THE
HIMALAYAN
MASTERS
SWAMI RAMA

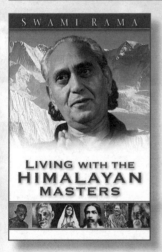

In this classic spiritual autobiography, hear the message of
Sri Swami Rama, one of the greatest sages of the 20th century.
As he shares precious experiences with his beloved master,
Sri Bengali Baba, and many other well-known and hidden
spiritual luminaries, you will have a glimpse of the living
tradition of the Himalayan Masters.

This spiritual treasure records Swami Rama's personal quest
for enlightenment and gives profound insights into the living
wisdom that is the core of his spiritual mission and legacy.
This living wisdom continues to enlighten seekers even
today, long after Swamiji's maha-samadhi in 1996, sharing
the timeless blessing of the sages of the Himalayan Tradition.

To order: 800-822-4547
Email: mailorder@HimalayanInstitute.org
Visit: HimalayanInstitute.org

HIMALAYAN
INSTITUTE®

Awakening Power
in the Yoga Sutra
VIBHUTI PADA

Vibhuti Pada, the third chapter of Patanjali's *Yoga Sutra*, is a treasure trove of wisdom and practice from the esoteric heart of the yogic and tantric traditions. For over 2,000 years, this text has been the definitive authority on unlocking extraordinary yogic powers hidden deep within our mind. Vibhuti Pada is revered as essential source wisdom on the dynamics of meditation and its role in unveiling the power of consciousness.

Awakening Power in the Yoga Sutra is the first practitioner-oriented commentary on Vibhuti Pada written for the modern seeker. Fully grounded in scholarly understanding, this commentary is brought to life through the direct experience of a modern-day master and is immeasurably enriched by the gift of experiential wisdom passed down to him through a living tradition—wisdom revealed in written form for the first time.

To order: 800-822-4547
Email: mailorder@HimalayanInstitute.org
Visit: HimalayanInstitute.org

The Secret of the Yoga Sutra
Samadhi Pada
Pandit Rajmani Tigunait, PhD

The Yoga Sutra is the living source wisdom of the yoga tradition, and is as relevant today as it was 2,200 years ago when it was codified by the sage Patanjali. Using this ancient yogic text as a guide, we can unlock the hidden power of yoga, and experience the promise of yoga in our lives. By applying its living wisdom in our practice, we can achieve the purpose of life: lasting fulfillment and ultimate freedom.

Paperback, 6" x 9", 331 pages
$24.95, ISBN 978-0-89389-277-7

The Practice of the Yoga Sutra
Sadhana Pada
Pandit Rajmani Tigunait, PhD

In Pandit Tigunait's practitioner-oriented commentary series, we see this ancient text through the filter of scholarly understanding and experiential knowledge gained through decades of advanced yogic practices. Through *The Secret of the Yoga Sutra* and *The Practice of the Yoga Sutra*, we receive the gift of living wisdom he received from the masters of the Himalayan Tradition, leading us to lasting happiness.

Paperback, 6" x 9", 389 Pages
$24.95, ISBN 978-0-89389-279-1

To order: 800-822-4547
Email: mailorder@HimalayanInstitute.org
Visit: HimalayanInstitute.org

Touched by Fire
Pandit Rajmani Tigunait, PhD

This vivid autobiography of a remarkable spiritual leader—
Pandit Rajmani Tigunait, PhD—reveals his experiences and
encounters with numerous teachers, sages, and his master, the
late Swami Rama of the Himalayas. His well-told journey is
filled with years of disciplined study and the struggle to master
the lessons and skills passed to him. *Touched by Fire* brings
Western culture a glimpse of Eastern philosophies in a clear,
understandable fashion, and provides numerous photographs
showing a part of the world many will never see for themselves.

Paperback with flaps, 6" x 9", 296 pages
$16.95, ISBN 978-0-89389-239-5

At the Eleventh Hour
Pandit Rajmani Tigunait, PhD

This book is more than the biography of a great sage—it is a
revelation of the many astonishing accomplishments Swami
Rama achieved in his life. These pages serve as a guide to the
more esoteric and advanced practices of yoga and tantra not
commonly taught or understood in the West. And they bring
you to holy places in India, revealing why these sacred sites are
important and how to go about visiting them. The wisdom in
these stories penetrates beyond the power of words.

Paperback with flaps, 6" x 9", 448 pages
$18.95, ISBN 978-0-89389-211-1

To order: 800-822-4547
Email: mailorder@HimalayanInstitute.org
Visit: HimalayanInstitute.org

Perennial Psychology of the Bhagavad Gita
Swami Rama

With the guidance and commentary of Himalayan Master Swami Rama, you can explore the wisdom of the Bhagavad Gita, which allows one to be vibrant and creative in the external world while maintaining a state of inner tranquility. This commentary on the Bhagavad Gita is a unique opportunity to see the Gita through the perspective of a master yogi, and is an excellent version for practitioners of yoga meditation. Spiritual seekers, psychotherapists, and students of Eastern studies will all find a storehouse of wisdom in this volume.

Paperback, 6" x 9", 479 pages
$19.95, ISBN 978-0-89389-090-2

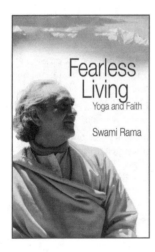

Fearless Living: Yoga and Faith
Swami Rama

Learn to live without fear—to trust a higher power, a divine purpose. In this collection of anecdotes from the astonishing life of Swami Rama, you will understand that there is a way to move beyond mere faith and into the realm of personal revelation. Through his astonishing life experiences we learn about ego and humility, see how to overcome fears that inhibit us, discover sacred places and rituals, and learn the importance of a one-pointed, positive mind. Swami Rama teaches us to see with the eyes of faith and move beyond our self-imposed limitations.

Paperback with flaps, 6" x 9", 160 pages
$12.95, ISBN 978-0-89389-251-7

To order: 800-822-4547
Email: mailorder@HimalayanInstitute.org
Visit: HimalayanInstitute.org

HIMALAYAN
INSTITUTE®

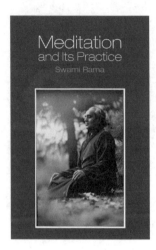

Meditation and Its Practice
Swami Rama

In this practical guide to inner life, Swami Rama teaches us how to slip away from the mental turbulence of our ordinary thought processes into an infinite reservoir of consciousness. This clear, concise meditation manual provides systematic guidance in the techniques of meditation - a powerful tool for transforming our lives and increasing our experience of peace, joy, creativity, and inner tranquility.

Paperback, 6" x 9", 128 pages
$12.95, ISBN 978-0-89389-153-4

The Art of Joyful Living
Swami Rama

In *The Art of Joyful Living*, Swami Rama imparts a message of inspiration and optimism: that you are responsible for making your life happy and emanating that happiness to others. This book shows you how to maintain a joyful view of life even in difficult times.

It contains sections on transforming habit patterns, working with negative emotions, developing strength and willpower, developing intuition, spirituality in loving relationships, learning to be your own therapist, understanding the process of meditation, and more!

Paperback, 6" x 9", 198 pages
$15.95, ISBN 978-0-89389-236-4

To order: 800-822-4547
Email: mailorder@HimalayanInstitute.org
Visit: HimalayanInstitute.org

HIMALAYAN INSTITUTE